Dani's Last Dance

By Glenda Head, R.N.
©2007

Order this book online at www.trafford.com/07-0917
or email orders@trafford.com

Most Trafford titles are also available at major online book retailers.

Note for Librarians: A cataloguing record for this book is available from Library
and Archives Canada at www.collectionscanada.ca/amicus/index-e.html

Printed in Victoria, BC, Canada.

ISBN: 978-1-4251-2682-7

*We at Trafford believe that it is the responsibility of us all, as both individuals
and corporations, to make choices that are environmentally and socially sound.
You, in turn, are supporting this responsible conduct each time you purchase a
Trafford book, or make use of our publishing services. To find out how you are
helping, please visit www.trafford.com/responsiblepublishing.html*

*Our mission is to efficiently provide the world's finest, most comprehensive
book publishing service, enabling every author to experience success.
To find out how to publish your book, your way, and have it available
worldwide, visit us online at www.trafford.com/10510*

www.trafford.com

North America & international
toll-free: 1 888 232 4444 (USA & Canada)
phone: 250 383 6864 ♦ fax: 250 383 6804
email: info@trafford.com

The United Kingdom & Europe
phone: +44 (0)1865 722 113 ♦ local rate: 0845 230 9601
facsimile: +44 (0)1865 722 868 ♦ email: info.uk@trafford.com

10 9 8 7 6 5 4 3 2

*Dedicated to Jack, Daniel, and Alyssa
in memory of their mother*

ACKNOWLEDGEMENTS

I owe a big debt of gratitude to my sisters Carol Barker and Alice Janssen for pouring over my first draft and making many helpful and insightful comments. My son Glen Head has been a constant source of encouragement. I am especially thankful to him and his partner, Doug Farrell, of Far Ahead Advertising, Inc. and to their ace graphic designer Eric Bradford for marshalling their resources and expertise in putting the book together. To my daughter Cami, daughter-in-law Shelly, and "Glenda's Goofy Gals," I say thank you for being such wonderful and constant cheerleaders as I waded through the process of putting my book together, a process that was both painful and healing. Dan, your steady urging to complete this project and your patient love has kept me going.

Most of all, I want to express my thanks to all of my loyal MailMax readers who wrote, called, and emailed me, urging me to write Dani's story in book form.

Part I

The Unreal Reality
of Cancer

Chapter 1

THE PREPARATION

When did it first hit me? That blinding insight? That awe-awakening knowledge that all of my plans...all of my schooling to be a nurse...all of my years of working at hospice...were not simply the fulfillment of a dream, of a destiny, as I had supposed, but were part of an eternal and divinely sovereign plan of preparation?

Perhaps my entire life had been a preparation for my most challenging role, but the real basic training began in 1989. I was in my mid-forties, a housewife and mother living in Benton Harbor, Michigan with my husband Dan, pastor of a small church. Our two oldest children, Danette and Glen, were married with families of their own and daughter Cami would graduate from high school within a few years. It was that year when Dan and I invited 94-year-old Hazel Pullen, a member of our church, to live with us. In retrospect I can see that that decision marked the beginning of my preparation in earnest.

Hazel was a diminutive, stooped lady with a crown of thick white hair, a dazzling smile and a zest for living. In spite of being nearly completely deaf and legally blind, she went on vacation with us, enjoyed fishing with Dan, and played miniature golf. Over the years as Hazel and I sat for hours talking, I was amazed at her wealth of wisdom and treasure trove of remembered experiences. I was mesmerized by her recounting of the many trips she had taken both here and abroad after her retirement in 1947. She was so independent that at age 83 she had climbed a ladder to replace some missing shingles on her roof. It was as I listened to this vibrant woman that I began to think, *if I live to be as old as Hazel, I'm just starting the second half of my life. What am I going to do to make those years count?*

During the final year of her life, Hazel experienced a steady decline in health. Then, at age 99, she was diagnosed with breast cancer and I, with the blessing of her niece, made the decision that she would remain in my home and I would take care of her until her death. Kathy Webster, a nurse and Director of Clinical Services at Hospice at Home, came to our house to admit Hazel to hospice. I didn't know a great deal about hospice at the time but soon learned that its role is to care for those who are dying and to provide support to the family. I had no nursing experience. Ours had always been such a healthy family, and I was certainly ignorant about caring for a dying person. After all, I'd "only" been a housewife and mother for the last twenty-some years. I felt so exhausted and inadequate as I cared for Hazel that when hospice nurse Lorraine Arend knocked on my door, I greeted her with tears of relief; and an immediate bond was forged between us. Surprisingly, Hazel died just two weeks after her breast cancer diagnosis, but Lorraine's impact on me was life changing.

I knew now what I wanted to do with the rest of my life; I would become a hospice nurse. And so it was that I drove out to our local college the week after Hazel's funeral, swallowed my fear and took the plunge into the great unknown. I walked over the threshold of the door into the offices of the nursing department and nothing has been the same since. I enjoyed being in a learning environment again and it was fun to interact with other students half my age, but it turned out to be far more challenging than I had anticipated. There were times when I felt I was hanging off a cliff by bloody fingernails as I tried to tackle the voluminous reading assignments, study for tests, work as a nursing assistant at Lakeland Hospital, participate in the various nursing rotations, keep my home life humming smoothly, stay involved in church activities, help out my newly-widowed mother, and deal with a mother-in-law who was having another major manic-depressive episode.

Finally, in the spring of 1997, I graduated from college with my nursing degree. I went to work immediately at Watervliet Community Hospital, where I gained valuable experience working on the medical and surgical floors and occasionally taking an extra shift in rehab or ICU. After 14 months at

Watervliet, I applied to work at Hospice at Home and spent the following six years there as a registered nurse, a supervisor, and a bereavement care coordinator, gaining insight and experience in the care of the dying and their family members. I loved my work, feeling that it was my niche in life to serve the terminally ill and their families. The variety of patients and families kept the work fresh and challenging for me, and I felt that my own life was immeasurably enriched by my hospice experiences.

In 2003, our oldest daughter Danette (nicknamed Dani) and her husband Kerry and three children were living in New Palestine, Indiana, four hours distant. Kerry had a business making beautiful hand-crafted custom saddles, and Dani worked as a unit secretary at Methodist Hospital in nearby Indianapolis. Our youngest daughter Cami was a social worker living and working in Chicago. Our son Glen, his wife Shelly and three children lived locally, where Shelly operated a daycare and Glen was co-owner of FarAhead Advertising which put out, among other publications, a weekly advertising paper for which I wrote a column.

We were a close-knit family and, although I had always been thankful that my family had been spared many painful ordeals that other families had had to endure, my work as a hospice nurse had brought me face to face with the unimaginable tragedies some families have endured and made me even more keenly aware of just how blessed we were. All that changed in an instant with one phone call. Never once had it entered my mind that all of my studying to become a registered nurse, all of my experience working in the hospital, and all of my years with hospice were ultimately preparation for caring for my own child. I chronicled that very personal journey in my MailMax columns and the entire community rallied behind our family with encouragement and support. What follows are, in large part, the many columns I wrote over the two year period that rocked our family, challenged me as a hospice nurse, and tested our faith in the goodness of God.

Chapter 2

THE PHONE CALL

In the final paragraph of last week's column, I said, "I want to make it my goal to worry less and enjoy life more." That was before the phone call. I had no idea when I wrote those words that I would be put to the test so severely and so quickly. When I got home from work Wednesday, the answering machine light was blinking, so I pushed the "play" button and heard my 38-year-old daughter's voice from Indianapolis, "Hi, it's Danette. Give me a call when you get home." It sounded so benign. There was no sense of trouble, no hint of anguish.

After supper, Dan called her. "I have cancer," she said, and with those three shocking words, our world was turned upside down. A year ago last January, Dani's doctor had found a lump in her breast during a routine examination. However, the doctor had assured her that it was probably just a cyst. "Give me a call if it gets bigger," she told Dani.

In early summer, Dani thought the lump might be a bit bigger. A visit to her doctor in late summer verified that it had, indeed, gotten larger and the doctor ordered a mammogram and an ultrasound. It wasn't until early November that Dani got the results. "Everything looks okay"" she was told. "It's just a cyst."

When she came home for Christmas, Dani confided in me that the lump was getting very large. I reminded her that fibrocystic breasts run in our family, and I encouraged her to have the fluid aspirated. When she saw her doctor in early February to have the cyst drained, the doctor took one look at the breast and refused to aspirate it because of its size. An appointment was scheduled for last Wednesday at the Breast Clinic at the Methodist Hospital in Indianapolis where Dani works.

When the nurse at the Breast Clinic saw the lump, she was astounded at its size. It was now huge and darkly discolored. She brought in some of her staff members to see it. All the while Dani was laughing and joking about the ugly sight. When the doctor came in, though, she was brusque to the point of rudeness. "Why didn't you come in earlier?" she demanded. Dani sputtered, "Well, I was told that the ultrasound confirmed it's a cyst, so I didn't think there was any urgency. I'm just here to get it drained." It was then that the doctor sat down, took Dani's hands, and said, "Well, that's not what I see. You have breast cancer." Within seconds, Dani's laughter turned to great sobs of disbelief and horror. The doctor took a biopsy, confirming the cancer diagnosis. The following day Dani saw a surgeon and on Friday she met with an oncologist. Monday she will begin about 10 months of chemotherapy, followed by a radical mastectomy. Wednesday she will have a series of scans to see if the cancer has spread.

I have spent the past few days doing just what I vowed not to do; I've been worrying about my "little girl." I've cried great buckets of tears from the very depths of my soul and have alternated between denial ("this can't be happening"), anger that it took over a year to make an accurate diagnosis, to a deep peace and confidence that God is still in control.

I've been reliving in my mind the special moments of Dani's life - the day she was born, her first day at school, images of her in her Brownie uniform, as Marcellus homecoming queen, as Miss Marcellus in 1982, as a guard on the championship Marcellus girls' basketball team, her

wedding day, the birth of each of her children. Now I wonder if those memories are all I will have left of my precious daughter.

Many friends and family have called or emailed to offer encouragement, and I have been buoyed up by the prayers of my hospice team, the Nazarene women's Bible study group where I spoke Thursday evening, by my own church family, and countless others.

So, I am writing this column for two reasons. One is to appeal to you as you are reading this to pray for Dani and her family (husband Kerry Shannon, son Jack, age 16; son Daniel, age 14; and 9-year-old Alyssa). The other reason is to urge you to follow through with having yearly mammograms (or encourage your loved one to do so) and to be aggressive if you have any suspicion of a problem. It has now been four days since the dreadful news and we are beginning to accept the reality, being challenged not to worry, to place it in the Heavenly Father's hands, and to continue to enjoy life because it is so very precious and so very, very short.

During that initial phone call with Dani, I was encouraged by the fact that her oncologist, Dr. Markham had been so thorough in his explanations to her. He spent about an hour with Danette and Kerry, recording the entire conversation. He also wrote the main points out on a white board that he then photographed; so when Dani went home, she had the tape and a 14" by 11" picture of his white board notes. As a nurse, I was well aware that when doctors give devastating news, patients and families very often hear only a fraction of what is being said as their minds try to grasp the reality of the situation. I was much reassured by Dr. Markham's thoroughness in educating Danette and Kerry. Dani contacted a physician friend of hers who does cancer research at Indiana University and he confirmed that Dr. Markham's strategy to treat the cancer was exactly right.

Later on the evening of Dani's call, I phoned our daughter Cami. Although Dani had already called her with the news, I needed to touch base with Cami myself and lend her some encouragement. Dani was nearly 15 years old and had accompanied Dan into the delivery room when Cami, our little surprise package, was born. There had always been a close bond between the two sisters. Now, I was concerned about how Cami, off in Chicago by herself, would handle this devastating news, though I knew that ultimately, she would be fine. A few hours later, our son Glen arrived on our doorstep. He and Dani had been forever buddies, growing up together on our small farm outside Marcellus, Michigan. We hugged and cried and then prayed together, each struggling to wrap our minds around the fact that the unthinkable had become a reality for our family. We made phone calls and sent e-mails to a number of friends and family that evening, so immediately we were strengthened by the knowledge that many others would be praying for Dani. Sleep did not come easily that night as the memories of her life swept over me. There was nothing about Danette's life that would predispose her to having cancer. She was not a smoker or drinker. She ate a healthy diet, even drinking a glass of freshly juiced carrots and apple each morning. She took a popular herbal supplement and vitamins and worked out regularly at the local family gym. I thought about the tough road of chemotherapy, surgery, and radiation that lay ahead of her; and I thought about the very real possibility that she might be fighting a losing battle. The reality we were facing seemed so unreal.

Meanwhile, down in New Palestine, Dani was having a restless night also and awoke repeatedly with bouts of nausea. Her first thought was, "This is it already. I'm going to die." Kerry would pray for her and hold her each time she awoke and then called Dani's surgeon first thing in the morning. The surgeon assured them that she was not dying but that she was suffering from anxiety and that this is very common with a new cancer diagnosis. The surgeon prescribed Xanax, an anti-anxiety medication, for Dani to take at bedtime and she was then able to get a good night's sleep.

Chapter 3
LAUGHING THROUGH
THE HARD TIMES

Two weeks ago in this column I shared with you my shock and anguish when I learned that my 38-year-old daughter Dani had just been diagnosed with breast cancer. I am happy to report that as the results of her various tests have come back, my hopes for a cure for her have soared. Despite the 14-month delay in diagnosis, her lab results were all normal. Apart from a spot on her liver about the size of two grains of sand (too small to biopsy), the bone and CT scans indicate that the cancer has not metastasized to major organs or to bone. A biopsy of a suspicious lump in the right breast was also negative. There is, however, some lymph node involvement. Her first chemo treatment, a combination of Taxotere and Adriamycin, left her quite sick for a few days with nausea, vomiting, and fatigue; but as the anti-nausea medications are adjusted, we are hoping that she will do better. She is now back at work part time as a unit secretary in an Indianapolis hospital.

Before all this good news began to pour in, Dan, Cami, and I drove to Indianapolis to spend the weekend with Dani and her family. One of the difficult aspects of this for Dan and me is that we live four hours away, so it was good just to be able to wrap our arms around our daughter. There were some tears, of course, over the weekend; but mostly we laughed and had a good time. Cami and I went shopping for a wig with her. Now THERE'S a good stress-reliever! We laughed ourselves silly over some of the coiffures. She looked amazingly like a human yak when she donned the first wig, a monstrous, wild-looking creation in various shades of blonde, brown and red. Only the horns were missing.

Earlier in the week, my 17-year-old niece Alice Follett had called the ladies of the church and arranged a shower of little gifts for Dani. We knew nothing about this until Alice, niece Monica Janssen, and my sister Alice showed up on our doorstep one night with two large laundry baskets full of beautifully wrapped gifts (many with encouraging or humorous sayings or Bible verses tucked inside) for us to take to Dani. She was touched by this generous gesture of love. One of the gifts was a wrapped book that had once belonged to Dani's Grandma Head. Inside was a photograph of Dani's daughter Alyssa as a baby sitting on Grandma's lap. This brought a nostalgic "Ohhh!" from Dani, until she thumbed through the book and discovered a small card and started laughing. The card read, "Please return this book to Alma Head." Since Grandma died five years ago, Dani quipped, "I think I'll wait awhile to return this."

Another gift was from my grandson, five-year-old Bobby. Dani was touched when she realized that her nephew had parted with a favorite monster truck poster. When I later recounted to son Glen how much Bobby's sacrifice had meant to her, he grinned sheepishly and said, "Well, we had to edit his choice a bit. The heading on the poster he wanted to send was 'GRAVEDIGGER.'" In spite of the morbid subject, we couldn't help laughing; and when I relayed this to Dani, she burst into her infectious laugh.

Being able to look on the light side of things has helped our family through a lot of difficult times in the past and this has been no exception. Dani said that when she told her family that she would have a radical mastectomy, followed by breast reconstruction surgery, they got a good dose of laughter when her 16-year-old son Jack volunteered to donate skin tissue from his derriere (my word, not his) for the reconstruction.

You readers have been wonderful! In the past two weeks I have received many calls, notes of encouragement, books, and even a video. Though the outlook is much better than it was two weeks ago, we still need your prayers as Dani faces a difficult year of chemotherapy, surgery, and radiation. Thank you all for your kindness.

Even before Dani was diagnosed with breast cancer, my husband Dan had been experiencing chest pain. In typical male fashion, he refused to see a doctor. After all, he was one of those people who never gets sick. In the weeks since Dani's diagnosis, though, the chest pain had worsened so finally, a month later, he relented and made an appointment with his physician who hospitalized him immediately. It happened to be Easter weekend. Initial testing failed to turn up any problems, so he was released from the hospital; but when he failed a stress test later in the week, an angiogram was ordered. So, for about a week in April of 2003, I was in a whirlwind of phone calls or emails to update family members, making arrangements for someone to take charge of the Sunday Easter service at church, touching base with Dani to keep apprised of her situation, and continuing to work part-time as Bereavement Care Coordinator at Hospice at Home. I often felt bewildered at this double whammy and wondered what was happening to our happy, healthy family. It was a great relief when the angiogram revealed that, although Dan had some arterial blockage, it was not significant enough to require angioplasty. Dan was doing better on the medication recommended by the doctor and once again Dani's fight against breast cancer became our major concern.

Throughout these weeks, I clung to the belief that feelings are not a reliable gage of how I am doing. My emotions could be all over the place on any given day, yet on a deeper level I knew that I was okay. In her 1969 book <u>On Death and Dying</u>, Dr. Elisabeth Kubler-Ross presented a model describing five stages that people work through in dealing with grief. Although initially applied specifically to grief defined as the normal response to the loss of a loved one by death, it is often applied now to any loss (such as a job loss) or any traumatic experience or tragedy. The five stages are: Denial and isolation, anger, bargaining, depression, and acceptance. The stages do not necessarily follow in sequential order and, in fact, may all occur in a single day.

For me the whole process of dealing with Dani's tragic cancer disease was experienced as more of a layered effect. For instance, I was in denial in the sense that from the date of diagnosis, I grappled with the I-just-can't-believe-this-is-happening aspect, while at the same time experiencing a degree of acceptance because I was well aware from my hospice experience that Dani's late diagnosis meant she would be fighting an uphill battle.

Anger often manifests as "why me?" but as I acknowledged that I had led a blessed life, I had to ask myself, "why not me?" Many times, though, I wished that it was me with cancer rather than Dani. I was angry that the diagnosis was not made 14 months earlier, but it was not an anger that was directed at any one person but it was, rather, anger at the circumstances. Many friends and family members were appalled by the fact that Dani's primary physician had not immediately ordered a mammogram or ultrasound or performed a biopsy as soon as she discovered the lump in Dani's breast. Although I understand that anger, as a nurse I had some empathy for this doctor who did not aggressively pursue a diagnosis. I knew that even the best health professionals are only human beings whose judgments can sometimes be wrong in spite of their years of school-ing and experience. I also knew that Dani's young doctor was new and inexperienced in her profession, and I believed that this terrible oversight would serve to make her a better physician. That is not to say that I was immune to brief spurts of anger, for I would give anything to be able to go back in time and do things differently.

I could be angry at myself because as a hos-pice nurse I was very well acquainted with the rav-ages of cancer, and yet I had not been adamant that Dani get a second opinion or demand a biopsy. The reason was simply that fibrocystic breasts are com-mon among the women in my family and there had been so many false alarms that I made an assumption that this would simply prove to be one more false alarm. I worked hard at not blaming myself because I knew it was a destructive force that would swallow me up and leave me without the emotional resources to continue working at hospice or to be strong for my daughter and her family.

Often in a situation like this, the anger is dis-placed. For instance, a family member might really be angry at God or even at the person who is ill; but those feelings of anger are directed toward someone else such as a pastor or another family member. For me, I experienced pricks of anger toward well-mean-ing individuals who tried to Monday-morning quar-terback the situation. "If only she had been on such-and-such a supplement." "She should have been her own advocate and demanded a biopsy when the lump was found." "She must have some sin in her life." "It's all a matter of faith. She just needs more faith." Those sorts of comments, placing the blame back on

Dani's shoulders, made me angry and defensive for my daughter. The truth is that bad things sometimes do happen to good people. The truth is that even those people who eat a healthy diet and exercise and take care of their bodies (as Dani did), can still develop life-threatening diseases. The truth is that absence of illness is not the litmus test of faith; how we handle ourselves in the face of illness IS.

At this point, I was doing no bargaining, simply because I felt I had no bargaining chip that was worth offering in exchange for my daughter's life. Long ago I made a decision to give back to my Creator and Lord all that I am and to use my life to serve him by serving others. Though I often fulfill that promise imperfectly and fall woefully short of even my own expectations of myself, still I have not deviated from that commitment. What could I possibly offer God now in return for Dani's life? Besides, after a month of chemotherapy, we knew the chemo was doing its job and a sense of optimism began to prevail.

Depression also was not an issue at this point because all of our thoughts were geared toward helping Dani fight this battle and being an encouragement to her. There was no room for depression.

Chapter 4

BALD IS BEAUTIFUL

It was exactly one month ago today (as I write this) that the phone call came from our daughter Dani informing us that she has breast cancer. I've had so many inquiries about her that I thought I would bring you all up to date. Two weeks after her initial treatment, Dani was shedding hair so quickly and in such large tufts that she had her husband Kerry shave it off. She is officially a baldy now. But bald is beautiful...at least on her it is. Her son Daniel made her a tongue-in-cheek offer of his sun visor and she laughed at his "generosity" envisioning just how little protection the visor would give her bald pate. She decided not to wear a wig just yet because it is so uncomfortable, but she's wearing hats or turbans instead. This has opened the door to conversations with many cancer survivors and health care professionals who have been very helpful and supportive.

Her second chemo treatment was last Monday, three weeks after the initial treatment. She met first with her oncologist who was very encouraged and very encouraging. He told Dani that with just the initial chemo treatment, her tumor had shrunk from 9 cm x 7 cm to 3cm x 3 cm! He was also no longer able to feel the lymph node he had felt at her initial visit.

With all of this good news, the doctor decided to bump her chemo from every three weeks to every two weeks. When these initial six treatments are completed, he will evaluate her for the surgery this summer rather than in January or February of next year as was originally planned. In addition, for the first time, he introduced the possibility of a lumpectomy rather than a mastectomy.

Despite all of the good news, Dani was again very sick with nausea and vomiting after her Monday treatment, but she rebounded a little faster than after her first treatment. On Tuesday, as she was sitting on the edge of her bed with her bald head down, feeling weak and discouraged after yet another round of wrenching vomiting, her son Jack went by her room, saw his mom, and poked his head in the doorway. "Hey, Mom, are you doing something different with your hair?" he asked. In the midst of her misery, Dani lifted her shiny dome and laughed at her comic son. His dose of humor must have been just what the doctor ordered because by Wednesday she felt well enough to go on a field trip with her third-grade daughter Alyssa. There she met the mother of another third-grader who is undergoing chemotherapy, so they had much to talk about.

Dan and I, of course, are very grateful for the good news and are confident that the stunning results are due to the countless prayers that have been offered up for Dani. Many people have told us that they are praying for her and have put her on prayer chains. We know that there are people around the world praying for our daughter and this is both humbling and exciting. Thank you again for your prayers and kind thoughts that have given us strength and encouragement for this journey we walk with our daughter.

Throughout Dani's illness and treatment, I felt a need to tell anybody and everybody who would listen. It was as though I could convince my own denying mind that Dani really was in a battle for her life if I just told her story often enough. I lapped up words of encouragement like a thirsty desert wanderer. Every night I went to sleep thinking about it, praying about it; and I awoke each morning thinking about it, praying about it.

Writing about Dani's treatment and allowing my MailMax readers to enter into this family crisis through my weekly column was also good therapy for me. All the while, I continued my work as Bereavement Care Coordinator for Hospice at Home, visiting patients and families in their homes, conducting grief support groups, and organizing a yearly memorial service. This, too, brought comfort as I was able to identify even more closely with the pain and grief of those families.

Chapter 5

THE LONG HARD ROAD

MailMax - June 7, 2003

Time for an update. It has now been about two and a half months since my daughter Dani was diagnosed with a 9 x 7 cm cancerous breast tumor. The road has been long and hard for her. After each treatment she has experienced nausea and vomiting for several days, leaving her weak and fatigued. She feels good for about four days and then it's time for the next chemo session.

Although she was only working part time at Methodist Hospital, she had to give up working altogether on her chemo weeks. The hospital has been very good to her, though, giving her paid time off so that she doesn't lose her medical insurance. They have also been flexible in scheduling her to work on the days when she feels good and have set aside a room where she can rest if she needs to.

I had not seen Dani since early April when she was just starting to lose her hair, but two weeks ago, Mom, my sister Carol and I went to visit her.

Because of my work with hospice, I have seen many women who are very sick with cancer. Even so, I felt blindsided by the onslaught of deep anguish and grief that assaulted my heart as I walked through the door and saw my beautiful bald daughter lying in a recliner, too weak and nauseated even to visit with us for long.

Dani has some numbness and tingling in her fingers, a common side effect of chemo, and finds it difficult to concentrate. One of the anti-nausea medications she takes leaves her vision blurred, robbing her of the joy of reading. Her skin is blotched and flaky and so tender that she cannot even wear makeup. "Sometimes I don't even feel like I'm human anymore," she told me one day when she was discouraged. The discouragement seems to be a frequent companion these days.

As we sat in her living room, I felt so helpless to ease the suffering of my "little girl." Aren't mothers supposed to make it all better? I remember the times when Dani was sick as a child and I would fix her hot chocolate. She'd cuddle in my lap as I rocked her rhythmically back and forth in the rocking chair, singing or humming. Eventually, she would fall asleep and wake up feeling better. No amount of hot chocolate or holding her or rocking her can help her now.

We visited with her only a few minutes, then hugged her, prayed for her and left for our Indianapolis hotel. When we returned the following morning, Dani was sitting up, eating pudding and was feeling much better, so it was with a feeling of relief that we returned home.

Since then, she has had an allergic reaction to the chemo agent Taxotere she has been receiving. The good news, though, is that the tumor has shrunk from its original size to 1-1/2 x 2 cm and her oncologist, Dr. Markham, is very pleased with those results. Because of the allergic reaction, he has switched her to two other chemo agents that will be administered at three-week intervals. Along with the Adriamycin she had been receiving, she will now be given Taxol and Cisplatin. In addition, he made some other adjustments in medications and the first of the new combination was administered last Thursday. Dani called today and said that she had not had any nausea and vomiting; and today she went on an 18-minute walk with her husband and even did a bit of shopping. This was great news!

She still has a long road ahead of her and we do not know at this point when her surgery will be scheduled. I have drawn great strength and encouragement from those who have called or written. Please continue to pray for Dani and her family as they tread this difficult path.

In mid-June my husband Dan made national news. He was returning in his pickup with a friend after an evening of fishing out on Lake Michigan when he noticed smoke coming from Benton Harbor. He was aware that there had been rioting in Benton Harbor the previous night, precipitated by the death of a 28-year-old African American motorcyclist who was killed when he crashed into a house while fleeing police. For many years, Dan had been meeting weekly with several other pastors for prayer at the Benton Harbor Street Ministries near where the rioting was occurring. When he saw the smoke that evening, he was concerned for the safety of Rev. Yvonne Hester who oversees the ministry and he wanted to make sure that the building had not been torched. As he drove south of where he perceived the riots to be taking place, he spotted a group of rioters only half a block away when he stopped at an intersection.

Suddenly Dan found himself in the wrong place at the wrong time as the rioters turned and began to pelt his truck with rocks and bottles. As he sped from the intersection, the truck's windows were shattered and the body of the truck was damaged by the blows of the rocks. Fortunately, though shaken, Dan was unharmed and his passenger sustained only minor scrapes and bruises. Within days the rioting was quelled, but because we had always lived a rather quiet, uneventful life, Dan's narrow escape in Benton Harbor, compounded by his recent hospitalization and Dani's cancer diagnosis, only served to heighten the surreal quality of our lives in recent months.

Meanwhile, the doctors in Indianapolis were pleased with Dani's response to chemotherapy and determined that the chemo treatments could be halted and, after a few weeks of recovery time, she would undergo surgery to remove the left breast. There was a feeling of cautious optimism that Dani would, indeed, beat the cancer.

Chapter 6

OPERATION LAUGHTER

Wednesday was a beautiful summer day and the morning had been peaceful, though some niggling apprehension lurked in the background as we anticipated Danette's modified radical mastectomy scheduled for 1:30 p.m. I sat on the swing outdoors at Dani's home that morning, remembering with a smile that when she was about twelve years old, she was such a tomboy that she once said that she didn't want breasts because then she wouldn't be able to run fast.

When we arrived at the hospital, Danette was taken almost immediately to a small curtained cubicle accompanied by her husband Kerry, while my husband Dan and I settled into the large waiting room. Other people clustered in family groups, waiting to hear how the surgeries of their loved ones had gone. There was almost a palpable feeling of anxiety in the room. Occasionally, a surgeon would appear and the family would lean forward expectantly in a semi-circle as if to entrap every word, every scrap of hope and good news the doctor might have to offer.

Our daughter's cancer diagnosis had come four months earlier and though the chemotherapy had left Danette weak and wracked with nausea and vomiting, she was, nevertheless, on the rebound and had been told that the results were "amazing." The oncologist had actually said, "Danette, it looks like you're going to make it." So now, with lighter hearts, we could turn our thoughts and prayers to the final phases of treatment, including surgery to remove the treacherous tissue.

Dan and I were eventually taken back into the cubicle with Danette and Kerry and we reminisced and watched the clock. The time for her scheduled surgery came and went. Her pastor arrived and we prayed for her and sang "Great is Thy Faithfulness." Still we waited. The anesthesiologist came in and started an IV and said that some emergencies had come in, so it would be awhile. We waited some more. At last, at 3:40 p.m., Danette was wheeled into surgery, but before she went, I said to her, "Remember to look on the positive side, Dani...you'll be able to run faster now." "Yeah," Kerry quipped, "But you'll be running in circles," (because only one breast was being removed.) So, she went off to surgery laughing.

As we returned to the waiting room, two young women were huddled together sobbing. Their 36-year-old brother had just been diagnosed with an inoperable brain tumor. Dan prayed for them and I made a quick visit to the chapel. After a very late lunch, we again took up our posts back in the waiting room. We waited. And waited. Finally, four hours after Danette was taken into surgery, the surgeon came to tell us that everything had gone well and that she saw no evidence of cancerous lymph nodes, though the biopsy report would not be back until Tuesday. Apprehension gave way to relief.

Dani was taken to the floor where she works as a unit secretary and less than 24 hours later, she was back home. She's had very little pain, looks good, and is counting the days until her hair comes back in. When the mastectomy is sufficiently healed, she will have six weeks of daily radiation, followed by reconstructive surgery. But the end is in sight...an end that is far more optimistic than the initial outlook, and we are so thankful for all of your prayers and kind wishes. They have made a difference.

In late July, before her mastectomy, Danette had driven to Benton Harbor to spend the weekend with Dan and me before leaving her three children with us for their annual week with Granny and PawPaw. It happened to be the weekend of the annual Venetian Festival in St. Joseph that draws thousands of visitors. On that gorgeous Sunday morning our church met with several other area churches for a combined service at Shadowland Pavilion, overlooking the placid blue waters of Lake Michigan with its pier and lighthouse. Dani attended the service, wearing a straw hat to protect her bald head from the sun. She seemed to draw fresh strength as she soaked in the beautiful view, worshiped God in the beauty of His creation, and enjoyed seeing many old friends for the first time since her cancer diagnosis. Later she commented, "Oh, Mom, that was so good for me. I have missed the lake so much!" It was good for all of us here in Michigan to have her back "home," too; and to see her looking so lovely and feeling so well.

Chapter 7

THE GRAND GRANDS

Mountains of laundry. Boxes of cereal, cartons of ice cream, cans of soda, packages of microwave popcorn, gallons of milk, sacks of cookies, and bags of Cheetos. Constant dishwasher loads. Trips to buy groceries. Trips to the beach. Trips to pick up videos. Swimming. Boating. Fishing. Tubing. Noise. Laughter. Pranks. And, yes, a few squabbles and tears, too. It was our yearly week for the grandchildren to visit. There ought to be a reward of some kind handed out to grandparents who survive such a week. When Dan and I were in our twenties, we were houseparents at a children's home, caring for up to 17 children at a time in our home. Now we shake our heads and wonder how we ever did it.

Our daughter Danette's three children were here while she was recuperating from her mastectomy, and son Glen's three were also here much of the time, as well as my nephew John Janssen whom we adopt as an honorary grandson for a week each year. The older boys are perpetual eating machines, so as long as I kept the refrigerator and pantry well stocked, they entertained themselves. They stayed up late every night and, for them, the crack of dawn usually didn't come much before noon. I didn't mind. This was their vacation, after all. They are all honor students and hard workers. Jack holds down three part-time jobs, helps around home, and plays sports. Daniel helps his father Kerry in his saddle-making shop, with lawn mowing, and was building himself a shelf when I was last visiting. Jack has his driver's license now, so I let him borrow my car a few times. By opening the sunroof and a quick change of CDs, the car was instantly transformed into a chick-magnet mobile. Glen's son, five-year-old Bobby idolizes his older cousins, so he was content just to swim and wrestle with the big boys.

Tuesday Danette called to say that she had seen her surgeon that day. The biopsy report indicated that there was no cancer in any of the lymph nodes and the lump that was removed was simply scar tissue. The surgeon was actually clapping as she told Dani that the chemo response was unprecedented in her 15 years of practice.

Thursday, I took Glen's daughters, Megan and Kaitlyn, and Dani's daughter Alyssa to St. Joe, where we went to Yore Favorite Things so that each girl could select a teacup. After getting a hot dog at the cart across the street, we took the dogs for a picnic on the bluff. It was a picture-perfect day overlooking the beautiful waters of Lake Michigan. Arriving back home, the girls donned their fancy formals and makeup and arranged their hair and we headed to Great-grandma Hogoboom's doll-filled house for our annual tea party.

Last night we returned the kids to their rightful owners. Danette had on a peach-colored blouse and matching scarf and she looked wonderful. Under the scarf she was sporting a "five o'clock shadow," and she's delighted that she is once again growing hair. Dan and I are simply relaxing today and listening to the sounds of silence. It was a good week, though. The grands are grand and they love us and think their PawPaw and Granny are "cool." There is no better reward.

41

After Dani had a few weeks to recover from her mastectomy, she began a series of radiation treatments. Since she had resumed her job at the hospital, she was able to simply take a short break and slip downstairs to the radiation department to receive her treatments. She remained cheerfully upbeat, buoyed by the support of her co-workers, friends, and family. She was doing so well by September, in fact, that Dan and I took a wonderful three-week trip to Great Britain with his sister Gloria and her husband Storey. While we were there, we visited many cathedrals, all of which had small books in which visitors could enter prayer requests. A group of members in each church would meet regularly to pray for the needs entered into those books.   And so, throughout England, Wales, and Scotland I wrote out my heart's desire to see my daughter completely healed of cancer. I found great comfort in knowing that Christians all across Great Britain were praying for Dani. Every chance I got, I would locate an internet café and email Dani and my other children to keep updated on family life back in the States.

Life seemed to be returning to normal for all of us. Dani was feeling stronger each day and was once again able to enter into family life with enthusiasm and was enjoying her work at the hospital. I was busy planning the Hospice at Home annual memorial service. Meanwhile, we were all anxiously awaiting the results of tests Dani was scheduled to have at the end of October. When tests and scans indicated that she was cancer-free, we were all elated.

Chapter 8

THE POWERFUL WINDSTORM

Yesterday was a beautiful balmy day here in Southwest Michigan, one of those days that makes you feel like all is right with the world. As I was heading home from my day at hospice, though, a powerful wind started to sweep through our area. When I turned down Waverly Street near my home, I gasped in delight. Ahead of me, for the length of the street, newly fallen leaves were being rousted from the ground by the wind and were dancing in the sunlight, swirling eddies, pirouetting in a joyful golden ballet.

Later in the evening as I sat in my favorite chair reading, I could hear the wind picking up speed, howling outside like a hungry lion. Turning on the light in the backyard, I watched the tops of our towering pine trees swaying wildly to and fro, tempestuous hula dancers caught in the act of celebration. To me, it was beautiful.

But, the wind also brought a sudden drop in temperature so that when I awoke this morning, the forecast for today predicted a high that was only in the 20s. Many of the yards that yesterday had sported blankets of leaves had been swept bare by the wind. Several trees in our neighborhood fell during the windstorm, all of them had been dead, or nearly so, before the work of the wind toppled them. Some of the hospice staff reported that wind damage had left them without power at their homes.

Today I have been pondering yesterday's unusual windstorm. I've been in a reflective mood anyway as Thanksgiving approaches, reliving in my mind the mighty storm that hit my own life this past year, bringing with it its own sudden chill. Of course, I am talking about my daughter Danette's breast cancer diagnosis last spring. She has since endured chemotherapy, had a total mastectomy, and just last month completed radiation. All of the reports are encouraging and she now faces reconstructive surgery sometime next year. She tires easily and has developed chemo-induced arthritis, but she is steadily gaining strength and stamina. How thankful we are that she is still with us to celebrate another Thanksgiving, that her infectious laugh and beautiful spirit will continue to grace our lives!

Just as yesterday's wind brought its own unique beautiful delights, Danette's illness revealed much that was beautiful. The strength of our family bond of love was affirmed as our emotions swayed to and fro with the winds of her illness. The kindness of family and friends brought delight to our hearts as the depth of their caring was manifested throughout the storm. Our hearts danced with joy with each increasingly optimistic report we received. The empathy we feel for other families who have faced cancer or other crises has deepened through the knowing that comes only through personally enduring the storm. Though we often felt powerless to help Dani, we were driven repeatedly into the arms of the Source of all power.

The mighty wind that blew into our lives brought destruction, too. Gone is our naïve confidence that cancer would never strike close to home and heart. Dead limbs of self-reliance have been pruned, as we've been forced to lean on others for encouragement and strength. Our priorities have shifted like autumn leaves in the storm as we were hit with the winds of change.

And now the worst of the storm has passed, and we have a profound feeling of gratitude as we approach this Thanksgiving season. But, what if Danette had not survived, I wonder. Would I still be thankful this year? Recently I came across a poem by Annie Johnson Flint entitled, "The Blessings That Remain." It's a reminder that even with the worst of losses, there are blessings that remain. In the midst of the deepest grief, a seed of thankfulness will, in due time, spring forth into new life. I hope that would be my attitude...but I am, nevertheless, fervently grateful that I have not been put to the test.

I wish God's blessing for each of you during this Thanksgiving season.

The entire family met in our home for Thanksgiving and again in December to celebrate Christmas. Both times were permeated with a profound sense of joy and thankfulness that we could all be together. Dani was feeling great and looked like a high fashion model with her short hair and svelte figure. She reveled in her renewed vigor and good health. Hope flourished.

In January of 2004, I returned to Indianapolis to take a friend for surgery at the University of Indiana and spent the night at Dani's celebrating Alyssa's birthday. In February my family met together again in Chicago, surprising me with a 60th birthday celebration. We had a great time together and Dani continued to amaze us all with her progress. She would be meeting soon with a plastic surgeon to discuss her options for breast reconstruction surgery that summer.

Chapter 9

SLEEPLESS IN INDY

MailMax - March 6, 2004

When I called my daughter Dani to tell her I would be in Indianapolis and ask if I could spend the night with her, she laughed. "Well," she replied, "Sure, but you need to know that Alyssa is having a slumber party for her tenth birthday that night. I don't know how much sleep you'll get." And so it was that Sunday after church, I picked up my friend Ann who was traveling to Indianapolis with me and headed south.

Ann is so kind-hearted that she had made a beautiful doll cake for Alyssa even though she had never met my granddaughter. After dropping Ann off at the home of her relatives, I arrived at Dani's just as Alyssa and her friends were polishing off their pizza. The girls oohed and aahed over Ann's cake and made me feel welcome by calling me Granny.

After supper, the girls moved into the living room and presented a karaoke show. I enjoyed watching their talented and enthusiastic performances, until they laid aside the karaoke microphone, put some lively music on and began to dance around the living room, arms and legs flailing in youthful exuberance. Alyssa gyrated over to her mother and held out her hand. "Come dance with me," she pleaded. "I can't, Honey," Dani apologized. (She is still regaining strength from her cancer treatments.) So, Alyssa moved on to me and asked me to dance. I didn't mind playing second fiddle, so I joined the girls, putting on such a show that Dani had tears of laughter running down her cheeks.

After the entertainment, Alyssa shepherded her guests into her dad's workshop. Kerry is a saddle maker who turns out exquisite hand-crafted saddles. He gave the girls medallions of leather and let them use some of his tools; so for an hour or so, the girls worked diligently making key chains, proudly displaying their creations when they finished. Of course, I had to get into the act, too, so I fashioned my own keychain.

About 9:30 p.m. the girls settled down in sleeping bags in the living room to watch the video, "The Princess Diaries," each fortified with a bowl of popcorn. I had been assigned Alyssa's bed, so I gingerly made my way across her bedroom floor, strewn with balloons, coats, backpacks, and stuffed animals, with only an occasional patch of carpet visible. Settling into bed with a book, I reflected that it seemed good to once again be in a house full of happy, laughing children. Sometime later 14-year-old Daniel returned from his friend's house and I heard Dani warn him, "Don't go into the living room. The girls are watching their movie." In typical big brother retort, Daniel replied, "I don't want to watch Princess Diarrhea anyway!"

At 11:00 o'clock the video was over. From the direction of the living room I could hear giggling, squeals, and exaggerated whispers, punctuated every few minutes with loud shushing sounds. Then, a little after midnight, I heard the voice of authority in the person of Kerry telling the girls it was time to be quiet. In the silence that ensued, I fell into a light sleep, only

to be awakened about 1:30 a.m. One of the girls was sick. Half an hour later, the parents arrived to take her home. Again silence reigned but I could not get back to sleep, so I picked up my book to read again, finally falling asleep about 4:00 a.m.

At 7:30 a.m., I heard the parents arriving to retrieve their daughters and a new day had begun. As I was eating breakfast, I heard Dani and Kerry laughing in the pantry. "What's so funny?" I called. "We both came to the pantry at the same time. I reached for the Ibuprofen just as Kerry was reaching for the aspirin," Dani explained.

I don't know why they call them slumber parties. Slumber parties are not about sleep. They're about forging friendships, bonding together in youthful joy, and making lasting memories. I may have missed a few hours of sleep, but I wouldn't have missed Alyssa's slumber party for all the ZzZzZs in the world. A good time was had by all, especially Granny.

When a person has fought cancer and come out the other side, as the initial euphoria of being declared cancer-free subsides, there is often a nagging sense of waiting for the other shoe to drop. Once the wall of invulnerability has been breached, every sniffle, every ache, every slight upset stomach, potentially portends the return of cancer. Even while living a full and happy, grateful life, that cloud of doubt often hovers in the background of the minds of every cancer survivor and every family member.

I'm not exactly sure when the first inkling penetrated my thinking that perhaps something was amiss with Dani. She began to call often and complained of feeling depressed and lethargic, totally uncharacteristic of her. For the first time, in March 2004, I accompanied her to an appointment with Dr. Markham, her oncologist. I found him to be a no-nonsense physician whom I came to appreciate and respect in the months ahead. From the moment Dani told him I was a hospice nurse, I felt he included me as a partner in my daughter's plan of care and treatment options. At this visit which centered on Dani's depression, Dr Markham's opinion was that she was suffering a form of post traumatic stress disorder and said that this was not uncommon in cancer survivors. He put her on the anti-anxiety drug Ativan; but even after several weeks on the medication, she reported no improvement. The depression, as it turned out, was a harbinger of things to come.

Chapter 10

LIFE'S SHORT

I stand at the kitchen sink at my daughter Danette's house and I'm surrounded by wilted and dying plants. I pluck off the dead leaves, water the plants from the tap, and use a soft cloth to wipe the dust from the drooping leaves before setting them back in their appointed places. With just that little bit of TLC, I know they'll be good as new in a few days. I wish it were that easy with Danette, I think to myself. A few days earlier, I'd driven down to New Palestine, Indiana, southeast of Indianapolis to give Dani and her family a little TLC.

She has been going through a rough time these past few months, fighting depression. She had commented, "I feel like I've been robbed of all my gumption." When daughter Cami went to visit Danette, she called me when she returned home. She was in tears, "Mom that just isn't my sister." When nothing seemed to help, Dani had the thought that if she could just get away for awhile to warm, sunny Florida, she'd revive. Although she had a wonderful time visiting her mother-in-law in Naples, she developed a nagging headache that wouldn't go away.

She returned home the following weekend so that she, her 10-year-old daughter Alyssa, and Cami could participate in the Walk for the Cure, a fundraiser for breast cancer research. She enjoyed the event immensely, walked the entire three miles without any problem, and seemed like her old self for the few hours she was there. She was greatly encouraged by walking alongside the hundreds of other breast cancer survivors.

Tuesday morning while at work at hospice, I received a phone call from Danette, saying that she had been vomiting and her oncologist had ordered an MRI of her head. The next day as I was sitting in the parking lot at Wal-Mart before leaving for an appointment with a grieving family, I received the call. "Mom, the breast cancer has metastasized and I have a tumor on my brain."

"Oh, Honey, what do you want me to do?" I asked. "Do you need me to come down there now?"

"I don't know," she responded. "I'm not sure what you could do by coming down."

It wasn't what she said but the quaver in her voice that made me respond, "I'm coming! I'll have to wrap up a few things here and I'll start out as soon as I can."

She burst into tears and choked out, "Thank you."

The instant after I hung up, my composure evaporated. I immediately phoned my friend and supervisor, Lisa Bartoszek, and sobbed out the news to her. Then I drove to Dan's office to tell him and son Glen about Dani's phone call before heading back to my office at hospice. I canceled my afternoon appointments and finished my office work in a teary fog, but bathed in the comfort of warm hugs and expressions of concern from my co-workers, then headed for New Palestine.

The decision was made by the radiation oncologist, Dr. Yeh, and oncologist Dr. Markham to treat the brain tumor with radiation and Dani was started on a steroid immediately to reduce the swelling in the brain. On Thursday I accompanied her to her radiation treatment and then met with Dr. Yeh as he explained the MRI. The tumor was a little over an inch and had infiltrated the right temporal lobe. Surrounding the tumor itself was fluid that covered nearly half of the right hemisphere of her brain. I asked the doctor the hard question. "Is there a reasonable expectation of cure?"

"She now has Stage IV cancer," he replied, "and there is no cure. However, I think we can control it with radiation and she can have a couple more years of good quality life." He said, in fact, that he had one patient who lived 8 years after radiation for a similar tumor before the cancer returned. Others, he admitted, died within the first year.

It was sobering

news. Later that evening, Danette came and sat on my bed to talk about what lies ahead for her and her family. She was wearing an old sweatshirt she's had for over ten years. The lettering on it is a take-off of an old Reebok ad campaign and it reads, "Life's short; Pray hard." How appropriate, I thought and was comforted by the knowledge that people all around the globe were praying for her. It was therapeutic for me to work hard physically, too, as during the next few days I kept busy catching up on mountains of laundry, vacuuming, scrubbing sinks and floors and, yes, reviving dying plants. It was also encouraging to see the improvement in Danette day by day as the effects of the radiation and steroid began to manifest...not to mention the effects of prayer. When I left for home yesterday, she was cheerfully fixing breakfast for everyone and ironing a pair of slacks for her son. That's something she couldn't have done just a week earlier.

Once again, I am struck by the fact that we never know what a day may hold. We want to make the most of whatever time Danette has left on this earth. Actually, her old sweatshirt proclaims a good plan for anyone's life. "Pray hard" because no matter how long you live, "Life's short."

When Dr. Markham informed us that Dani had a brain tumor, he stated, "I know you hate to hear me say it, Dani, but I'm going to have to put you back on Decadron." Actually, she was looking forward to resuming the corticosteroid. When she had taken this potent drug the previous summer while undergoing chemotherapy, she seemed to have boundless energy and experienced a sense of euphoria. She was hoping that the Decadron would pull her out of the lethargy and depression she had been experiencing.

Decadron seems initially to be a wonder drug and is almost always prescribed in the case of a brain tumor in order to reduce the swelling of brain tissue. I once had a patient with a brain tumor who seemed at death's door when I made my initial visit. After being placed on Decadron, he rebounded and lived for several more months and was able to get out to restaurants, attend church, and go shopping with his wife. Unfortunately, this and other corticosteroids can have potent side effects such as depression, muscle wasting, and suppression of the adrenal glands. In a terminally ill patient, the benefits are usually deemed to outweigh any long-term side effects.

On the evening of the devastating news that Dani's breast cancer had metastasized to her brain, a group of men from their small church gathered with Kerry and Dani in their living room to encourage the couple. One of the men confessed, "Honestly, I was thinking, 'Come on, Danette, God has healed you. You ought to be rejoicing and instead you're depressed.' I am so sorry for judging you. Will you please forgive me?" Of course, Danette readily forgave the man, and his honest humility left a lasting impression on me.

When I returned to my job at hospice the following week, I had already made up my mind that I would tender my resignation in order to make myself available to Danette and her family. On my final day at work, my team gave me a wonderful send-off in the morning, followed by an afternoon gathering of all three Hospice at Home teams. I could not say enough good things about these special people who are dedicated to giving care to the dying and their families. More than most, they understand the pain of losing someone you love, and they rallied around me on that day in May with many words of encouragement. Some had donated their days off to me and the group presented me with several hundred dollars to help with travel expenses. What a blessing that was!

The phone calls flew back and forth between New Palestine and Benton Harbor as Dani kept me updated. When we weren't on the phone together, I was on the road, headed south to take her to her many appointments. Because the brain tumor meant a possibility of seizure, it was unsafe for her to drive; but Kerry couldn't always afford the time off from his saddle making to take Dani to her appointments. I was happy to do this because I then had the opportunity to hear first-hand all that the doctors were saying.

Chapter 11

GOOD MEDICINE

This is one of those weeks when everything seems to be going well, a week of fun and good news. I have my grandchildren for their annual week's vacation at Granny and PawPaw's house here in Benton Harbor. Danette's two oldest boys were only able to come for two days this time because Jack has a job now and Daniel is taking a summer physical education class. I knew that sooner or later this would happen, but it's a bittersweet transition. I had just been reflecting that it seems like Daniel just started kindergarten. I remember asking him what his kindergarten teacher's name was and he told me that it was Mrs. Paper. "That's a strange name," I replied. "I don't think I've ever heard the name Paper before." Walking through the room at that moment, Danette smiled and said, "It's Mrs. Page, Daniel, not Mrs. Paper." Now, after what seems like a fast-forwarding of the years, he's going into tenth grade and brother Jack will be a senior, making college plans.

Daniel brought a friend with him. Nate is a 6 foot, 4 inch boy just going into ninth grade. Cousin John Janssen, who just graduated from Watervliet High School, is also here, so there is a quartet of teenage eating machines camped out in our basement. Instead of the flicker of a campfire, they're camped around the flicker of the television set. After I brought the boys home, I went to the grocery store at 10:00 o'clock last night with a list of snacks Jack had given me at my request, and I spent $50 stocking up on goodies for the boys. I purchased things that every growing boy needs, like HoHos and cheese popcorn, Ding Dongs and Moose Tracks ice cream, Twinkies and Mountain Dew...you get the picture. Today at about 3:00 p.m. Jack informed me that they were out of snacks!

The younger girls have been trying on dresses for our annual tea party with my mother, whom they refer to as Grandma Huggy, and, along with 6-year-old Bobby, have been happily splashing in the pool or throwing water balloons at each other. I enjoy listening in on their conversations as they play. Children have such a unique perspective of things. Recently, as we were driving in the car, the voice of CeCe Winans floated out from the CD player as she sang Alabaster Box. Alyssa, who was in the backseat, piped up with concern in her voice, asking, "Is she swearing, PawPaw?" Her parents had obviously trained her that a word resembling "alabaster" is not appropriate for a young lady to say.

Since my son Glen and his wife Shelly are vacationing in Mexico, they prepared T-Bags for each of the children, a tradition I had stolen from my friend Kathy McNally years earlier to use with our own kids whenever we went on vacation without them. T-Bags are simply paper grocery sacks containing a few small wrapped gifts. On days with a "t" (Saturday, Tuesday, Thursday), the children are allowed to open one of the gifts. This creates an air of anticipation and excitement and lets them know that their parents are still thinking of them.

Although it's been great having my grandchildren around, the best thing about the week was my trip to Indianapolis to take Danette to her scans and latest doctor's appointment. She is unable to drive herself because of the brain tumor and her husband cannot take the time off work to accompany her to all of her many appointments. The good news is that the MRI of her brain showed that the tumor has shrunk from 2.7 cm. to 1.1 cm. The CT scan of her liver showed that the two suspect lesions have not changed and remain smaller than a grain of sand. So, there will be no further treatment at present as the radiation continues to do its work. She'll have another scan in two months.

There was also good news from some medical tests my mother (Grandma Huggy) had had done, so we are all breathing a little easier. Proverbs says, "A cheerful heart is good medicine," so I feel I've had a good dose for the week. I hope you have, too.

59

All the while that I was traveling back and forth to take Dani to her various appointments and then taking care of my grandchildren for their annual week of summer fun with Dan and me, we were in the final stages of preparing for a big family reunion that Dan and I were hosting over the Fourth of July weekend. Although this created an added pressure, it also was a welcomed diversion and both Dan and I felt buoyed by the success of the reunion and the warm collective embrace of love and concern we sensed from his cousins.

Then in early July after the reunion, I drove Dani and Alyssa to Pigeon Forge, Tennessee so that Alyssa and her friend Capri could perform their duet "You've Got a Friend in Me" in the Rising Star singing competition. We were able to take in some of the shows and tourist attractions, and the time away was a distraction for all of us, as well as a memorable three generation get-away.

Until Dani learned that her cancer had metastasized to the brain, she had not experienced any anger regarding her illness. She was initially in such a whirlwind of activity with tests, chemotherapy, radiation, and the mastectomy, that she didn't have time to entertain anger. All of her efforts were put into waging war against the disease, fully believing she would win the battle. Then there had been the tests in late October that indicated that she had, indeed, won her fight, leading to months of joyful gratitude.

Now that she knew her life was limited, though, she was very angry that the cancer hadn't been caught sooner, primarily because she now realized that she would not live to see her children grown and married. She would not be able to finish the job of raising her children to adulthood. Wanting to express that anger in a tangible way, she asked me to drive her to the local Goodwill store one day. There she purchased several different plates and bowls. "What are you planning to do with these?" I asked. "I'm going to smash them one by one against the side of the shed and then I'm going to collect the pieces and cement them onto a small tabletop, making a mosaic design. I'm mad now, Mom," she said, "and it's the best way I can think of to work out my anger." We took the box of used dishes home, but somehow she never got around to her anger project.

When Alyssa told me that she was angry that her mother's cancer was back, I asked her how she was handling her anger. "I go into the backyard with a bat and hit apples from the apple tree until I feel better," she said.

Although I wouldn't have said that I was angry, I do remember one clear incident of displaced anger. My sister Alice had called me at a particularly vulnerable moment one morning when I had been crying. "How are you doing?" she asked in concern. "Oh," I sarcastically snapped, "I'm doing just great! My daughter's dying and I can't do a thing about it! Of course, everything is just wonderful!" Surely my sister didn't expect or deserve such a reaction from me, and I felt terrible the moment the words were out of my mouth. I really was not upset with Alice, but she got the brunt of an anger that I hadn't even known was there. Even today, I would be hard-pressed to say just who or what was the real object of my anger, except that in that moment I was probably feeling quite overwhelmed with anticipatory grief, the grief that often assails a family member before their loved one has even died.

After the brain tumor diagnosis, Dani again began to receive many cards and letters. She had saved every single communication she had received since she was first diagnosed with breast cancer. When someone included a Scripture verse or a saying that was meaningful to her, Dani would copy it into an "encouragement notebook." Over and over again she would read through these tidbits of hope, support and cheer to bolster her flagging spirits.

Chapter 12

THE ROLLER COASTER RIDE

I've often heard it said that having cancer is like a roller coaster ride because of all of its ups and downs. I can attest to the accuracy of that comparison since my daughter Danette was diagnosed with cancer last year. The engine that runs the roller coaster ride is the reports from various tests. The ride to the top runs along the twin tracks of hope and good news, while the descent to the bottom runs on parallel tracks of fear and bad news.

Obviously, when we learned that her breast cancer had metastasized to the brain late last April, it was a breathtaking plunge to the bottom. Two months later when the scans showed that the tumor had shrunk to less than half its size with a single radiation treatment, we soared to the top again. We've been riding atop the roller coaster all summer, and it has been an especially joyful summer for Danette and her family. Bob, the head nurse on the unit at Methodist Hospital where Dani works, his wife Sandy, and the hospital staff flew Dani, her husband Kerry, and their three children to Florida for a vacation in June. They provided an SUV, a condominium, a day at Busch Gardens, and spending money. When the family arrived at the condo, there were welcoming banners signed by hospital staff members, along with an anniversary card from her co-workers. They had also arranged a moonlight dinner cruise for Dani and Kerry since they would be celebrating their 21st wedding anniversary that week. It was a wonderful, relaxing week for the entire family. When she got tired, Dani would simply lie down, whether it was on a park bench at Busch Gardens or aboard the cruise ship after dinner. The outpouring of care from her friends at the hospital was heartwarming.

Monday I headed back to Indiana to accompany Dani to another MRI scan. Other than general weakness and muscle pain, she has felt really good. She has been discouraged, though, about putting on weight after going on the corticosteroid Decadron, developing a "moon face" appearance common with steroid use. As I sat in her kitchen talking with her, I noticed a Styrofoam coffee cup from a local convenience store. Danette brought the cup over to me for closer inspection. I saw then that her husband had penciled on the cup, "You are going to be alright and skinny, starting right after this donut. Love, Kerry." I think his note probably cheered her more than the cup of coffee and the doughnut.

As we sat talking about all that has happened this past year and a half, Dani said, "Mom, I just feel like I'm in a free fall. Nothing about my life is in my control anymore. Sometimes I long for just one day to be a kid again, to be running in the field or playing kick the can at night, with not a care in the world."

We were all anticipating that Tuesday's MRI would indicate further tumor shrinkage. But, it was not to be. Instead, we were thrown for a loop and sent into a steep plummet once again. The scan clearly showed that the brain tumor had grown to nearly its original size, and the doctor said that surgery was now the treatment of choice.

Later that afternoon, as we were still adjusting to the latest report, Danette received a call from the doctor's office, stating that the surgeon had looked at the scans. It was his judgment that the questionable area in the brain was probably radiation necrosis (dead tissue from her radiation treatment) rather than cancer. Although we didn't exactly soar to the top of the coaster, we definitely were on our way up from the depths with this word of hope. The doctor ordered a PET scan for Danette next Monday to clarify the mass.

The good news is that our daughter Cami will drive Dani up here to Michigan immediately after the scan and the girls will spend five days with us. Dani wants to go fishing with her dad, ride on the Kal-Haven bike trail, and she is looking forward to going to Marcellus with Cami to spend time with her old school chums. As for me, I'm going to do everything I can to make this week a "top of the roller coaster" week for all of us. Then I will take Dani back to New Palestine on Friday and the following Monday we'll see the doctor for the PET scan report. Regardless of the roller coaster ride we've been on, our comfort is in knowing that the safety bar of faith is firmly snapped in place.

Chapter 13

MAKING RAINBOWS

I love rainbows! A couple of times during our June rains this year, I peeked outside when the sun was breaking through to see if I could spy a rainbow. There were none. Then in July when the rains ceased and I had to resort to watering my flowers myself, I couldn't help but smile at the little rainbows created by the spray of water. Sometimes you just have to make your own rainbows, I thought.

My daughters Danette and Cami were vacationing with Dan and me last week and we were counting on beautiful weather here in Southwest Michigan to make the week perfect. On Monday, though, the weather report was calling for a chance of showers with unseasonably cool weather every day that week. Since Monday was supposed to be our clearest day, as soon as the girls arrived late that afternoon, we headed immediately to go fishing.

It was a beautiful evening and Lake Michigan was smooth as glass. We were out in deep water for an hour or so when suddenly Danette's fishing pole began to bob. It took her awhile and she wasn't sure she'd have the strength to wrestle the fish in, but eventually she landed a 34 inch 17 pound salmon. Some time later, Cami snagged a 24 inch 8 pounder, and the girls were thrilled with their success. Dusk was approaching as we headed back to terra firma and we were treated to a gorgeous Lake Michigan sunset.

The weather for the rest of the week turned out to be exactly as forecast, but in spite of the less-than-hospitable Michigan weather, we chose to "make our own rainbows." There was the rainbow of our usual sisters' get-together, a monthly dinner at a local restaurant with my mother and four of my sisters who live in Southwest Michigan. This time we decided to include our daughters and daughters-in-law for the occasion. We had a great time catching up on each other's lives! There was also a special poignancy to the occasion as it was on everyone's mind that this might be the last opportunity to spend time with Danette.

MAKING RAINBOWS

On another day, a couple of Danette's friends from her days of working as a secretary in a local business took her out to lunch; and later Cami drove Dani to Marcellus to have dinner with some of her old school friends. These were precious "rainbow" times with special friends from the past. The memories were sweet.

There was the visit to a local produce stand to pick up some of our area's wonderful fruits and vegetables. This was a "rainbow" for Danette, who commented that there aren't any such stands in her area. There was the "rainbow" family time when son Glen and his family treated us all to lunch at a beautiful restaurant overlooking Lake Michigan. We had hoped to go bike riding on the Kal-Haven trail that afternoon, but by then Dani was not feeling up to it. Instead, we drove into St. Joe for ice cream cones and a walk around town to get an up-close look at the wonderful carrousel horses lining the summer streets.

Even though the weather was dreary for most of the five days the girls were here, we man-aged to "make our own rainbows," having a great time just enjoying the simple pleasures of life...good food and good fellowship. We slept late every day, spent long hours talking, and the girls enjoyed being back in Southwest Michigan. They have both missed the beauty of this area since moving away.

Friday night Cami returned to Chicago where she'll begin her master's program at Loyola University and I drove Dani back to Indiana. On Monday I took her to her doctor's appointment where we were advised that a number system is used with PET scans and anything over 3.5 suggests the probability of cancer. Dani's score from the recent scan of her brain was over 12. Now we await a visit with the neurosurgeon to determine what the next course of action will be. I suspect we'll have to create a lot more rainbows in the days ahead.

In the meantime, I hope you'll have a rainbow kind of week, even if you have to make a few small ones yourself.

69

Chapter 14

THE BRACELET

MailMax - September 18, 2004

Labor Day, Monday, September 6, fell this year on my daughter Danette's 40th birthday. As I prepared to return to Indianapolis the following day, I debated whether to give her the sapphire bracelet I had purchased as a birthday gift or whether I should wait to give it to her when I could take her out for a celebratory lunch. As I mulled it over, I was reminded that 40 years earlier, she was wearing another bracelet, a plastic name tag placed around her tiny wrist a few minutes after she first made her squalling appearance in this world. What a joyful, much-anticipated event her birth was! Somewhere tucked amongst other memorabilia, that bracelet still is testimony to that joyous occasion.

This occasion, however, would not be so joyous. My husband Dan, daughter Cami, and son Glen, along with his wife Shelly, were heading to Methodist Hospital in Indianapolis Tuesday morning to be present for Dani's brain surgery. The previous Friday I had accompanied her to see the neurosurgeon, Dr. Hall. He was very frank with us, stating that the surgery was risky because the tumor was deeply imbedded in the white matter of the brain. She could die on the operating table, or she could suffer a stroke. Since she had been experiencing increased pressure in her head, though, she did not hesitate to opt for the surgery. It was scheduled for Tuesday, September 7, the day after her 40th birthday.

When we arrived at the surgical waiting room at the hospital, we saw Dani's husband immediately and it wasn't until we greeted him that we noticed Danette lying on the sofa. My heart went out to her. It was obvious that she was not feeling well and it had been a difficult weekend fraught with fears and anxiety for her and her family as they anticipated Tuesday's surgery. Indeed, it had been a difficult weekend for all of us as we grappled with the prospect that Tuesday might be Dani's final day on earth...or that she might be left with major impairments. My mom had sent along a pair of pillowcases she had cross-stitched as a birthday gift for her, so I gave Dani that package, along with my gift of the bracelet. The gifts brought a smile to her face, which otherwise showed the signs of strain. I noticed she was already wearing her hospital name bracelet.

Everything occurred right on schedule and we gathered around her in her pre-op cubicle, laughing and joking. The mood was light and the nurse who came to attend Danette seemed surprised and commented, "I don't usually see this reaction from my families." Before Dani was taken for another CT scan, we took the time to pray for a successful surgery. After the scan, she was whisked off to surgery, but not before each of us had a chance to hug and kiss her. I cannot even begin to describe how that moment felt as I embraced my daughter and affirmed my love for her, not knowing if I would ever see her alive again. We were a solemn group heading back to the waiting room, not daring to look at one another for a time, knowing the pain we'd see reflected back in each other's eyes.

Danette's pastor and his wife and another friend joined us in the waiting room and the moments ticked by as we chatted, helped ourselves to drinks from the courtesy counter, and kept an anxious eye on the clock. Two hours later, the neurosurgeon joined us and said, "It went about as I expected. The mass was composed of some necrotic tissue, but there were also many viable cancer cells. She will need to follow up with radiation treatments. But, she is doing well and is responding to our questions appropriately." What relief! God had heard our prayers and Dani's life had been spared.

A short time later we were able to visit her by twos in the neuro intensive care unit. She was groggy and her head was swathed in bandages. When Glen was in with her, he said she brought a smile to the face of a new doctor who was asking Dani a number of questions about her medical history. "Do you have high blood pressure?" "Are you diabetic?" "Have you ever been treated for heart problems?" After a number of these questions, to which the answer was "No," Dani summed it all up, telling the physician, "I don't have anything the matter. I'm really a very healthy person." She doesn't remember that conversation; but she does remember and was deeply moved by the fact that after the doctor left her cubicle, her brother quietly sang over her, "The Lord Bless You and Keep You." By the following morning, she was doing so well that she was transferred to the VIP suite in that unit, a perq because of being employed by the hospital. She was soon bored and wanting to go home; and so, after another 24 hours, she was discharged. She looks wonderful and, except for a small scar in her right temple and one on her forehead, you'd never guess she'd had brain surgery only two days ago. It didn't take her long after she got home to snip off her hospital name bracelet.

Hopefully she will have many occasions to wear the birthday bracelet I gave her and, even though the long-term prognosis still is not good, we are rejoicing that we have her with us awhile longer. Maybe she'll even be around to celebrate a few more birthdays.

A few days after Dani's surgery, I drove her to a cancer survivor support group. She had never before been interested in such a group because her life was so full that she didn't feel the need. Now, however, she seemed both increasingly restless and increasingly depressed about her prognosis and wanted the support of others who were fighting their own battle with cancer. The facility where the group met was lovely and peaceful, and the group leader was encouraging. She showed us boxes of pictures cut from magazines and explained that we would be making large postcard collages later in the meeting and pointed to several hanging on the wall that had been made and framed by other participants. Then she led a discussion on cancer's psychological effects.

Throughout the discussion, Dani was distracted and seemed unable to sit still. She grabbed a box of the pictures from the coffee table and began to noisily riffle through them. At one point, she flicked a picture upward, snagging her earring which went sailing behind the sofa. She seemed totally oblivious to the fact that her behavior was a distraction to the group. Finally, the leader suggested a break, and when I was able to be alone with the leader in the kitchen, I apologized for the disturbance and said, "I think it's either too early or too late for Dani to be here." She was very understanding and encouraged us to stay to put together our collages; so after cookies and hot tea, we sat around a table with the other group members to work on our projects. At this point, the leader asked Dani about her family and, as Dani began to talk about her children, she became focused for the first time during the meeting. She proudly talked about each child and expressed her grief in knowing that her terminal diagnosis would mean leaving her children motherless. When she went back to trying to work on the collage, she again seemed unable to focus on the task at hand, so after retrieving her earring from behind the sofa, we left. We never returned.

It was during these first weeks after Dani's surgery that she and Kerry asked me to accompany them to their attorney's office, where they both signed their wills. Dani also signed a power of attorney and a living will, spelling out her preferences for medical care should she be unable to make those decisions herself. I was proud of Dani for having the foresight to take care of these practical matters.

During the week before Danette's surgery, Dan told me that he was experiencing some black flecks in his eye. With everything that was going on at the time, he felt he was too busy to see the eye doctor. However, as we waited in the waiting room during Dani's brain surgery, he mentioned the vision problems to our son Glen who had worked in the eye care business several years earlier. At Glen's insistence, right there in the waiting room, Dan called to schedule an eye appointment.

Chapter 15

WHEN IT RAINS, IT POURS

For the second time in eight days, I found myself sitting in a hospital waiting room with my son Glen by my side as a loved one was undergoing surgery. This time the patient was my husband Dan and the hospital was South Bend's St. Joseph Hospital. Glen and I had caught up on each other's lives, chatted with the talkative volunteer, drunk coffee from Styrofoam cups, watched the latest news on Hurricane Ivan, and read, all the while glancing at our watches as we waited for word on Dan's surgery.

Just the previous day, I had been in New Palestine, Indiana, with our daughter Danette. She was doing remarkably well. The day following her release from the hospital, we went shopping! With some creative hair styling, no one would ever guess that she'd had brain surgery just three days earlier. But, outdoors, a gust of wind rearranged the hairdo, revealing the surgical scars, and blowing away any illusion of health. Even though she had daily bursts of energy, these were quickly followed by exhaustion and weakness that would send her back to bed or to the recliner for hours at a time.

On Tuesday, one week after the surgery, she was in the kitchen baking chocolate chip cookies for her husband Kerry. It was his birthday and chocolate chip cookies were his favorite. Outside the sky was overcast and showers were predicted. "We need the rain and I can't wait for it to get here," Dani commented. She's always loved rainstorms and was looking forward to a refreshing downpour.

When the phone rang, I answered it. Dan's voice said simply, "Can you come home?" I felt an immediate sense of panic. "What's happened?" I asked. He quietly explained that he'd had showers of his own. His were showers of black spots in his right eye, accompanied by flashing lights and an encroaching curtain of black. After consulting a local eye doctor, he was told that he had a detached retina, a serious eye problem that would result in blindness without surgery. An appointment was made for Dan to see a specialist in South Bend the following morning, with surgery to follow in the afternoon.

After assuring Dan that I would be home that evening, I returned to the kitchen and explained the situation to Kerry and Danette. Then we circled up, with clasped hands and conjoined hearts as Kerry prayed for Dan. I went to pack my things and as I did so, I could hear the patter of rain on the roof. Returning to the kitchen, my heartstrings were pulled as I noticed the tears in Dani's eyes. She headed for the door and said, "Come on. I need this rain." I followed her out through Kerry's saddle-making shop and into the rain. She perched on the picnic table and began to sob. Since I was heading home and didn't want to get drenched, I quickly dashed back into Kerry's shop and covered myself from head to foot in a cape fashioned from one of the plastic sheets he uses to protect his saddles in shipping.

Looking like a wraith as the plastic billowed out behind me, I joined Dani on the picnic table and spread the sheet to cover her, too. I put my arms around her as the tears of heaven poured down to mingle with her own tears. After awhile, I asked, "The last straw?"

She shook her head yes, "Plus," she said, "he's my daddy and he's always been strong and healthy. I don't like to see this happening." As we sat there commiserating in the warm rain, Dani's daughter Alyssa arrived home from school. Seeing her mother crying, a look of fear crossed her face, so we gathered her under our shelter and together we huddled, united in love for one another and for a husband, father, and grandpa who needed us to be the strong ones now. As I looked out at the pouring rain, I thought, "When it rains, it pours," and I felt the helplessness of needing to be in two places at once.

Dan's surgery yesterday was successful and the doctor has given him an excellent prognosis, but for the next four weeks, he has to remain face down for 18-20 hours a day in order for the eye to heal and he will be off work during that time. His major concern has not been for himself, but for the disruption in the lives of so many who count on him. I tell him that it's just his turn for a little TLC. And, as for the rain, isn't that what makes things grow? I guess we are just in the growing season right now.

I felt so torn about being back in Michigan. I knew my husband needed me but I also felt that Dani and her family needed me, especially since the cloud of depression seemed to be settling in on her. The Decadron was having the opposite effect on her than it had had the previous summer when she had experienced euphoric energy. We kept in contact with frequent phone calls, and Dan recovered more quickly than his eye surgeon had predicted. I was able to return to Dani's home for the October 9 Making Strides against Breast Cancer walk in Indianapolis. She thought it was a mile-long walk and since we walked that distance regularly at a local park, she was excited about doing it with Alyssa and me. As it turned out, the course was three miles and I was concerned about whether she would be able to finish. Just as she was ready to give up, though, we realized the finish line was near. It was a tremendous boost to Dani's confidence to complete the walk and she beamed as we crossed the finish line. She slept the rest of the afternoon.

The following weekend we were sponsored by some of the oncology radiation nurses to attend a breast cancer survivor's luncheon/fashion show at a local hotel ballroom. It was amazing to see the large room filled with breast cancer survivors and Danette enjoyed visiting with the other survivors at our table, experiencing an instant rapport with these women. The affair was emceed by a local television personality and everything was done with such excellence that it was a beautiful moment in the lives of survivors and their caregivers who had experienced all too few beautiful moments since their cancer diagnoses.

Chapter 16

FRAMED

It's been a rough couple of weeks for my daughter Danette. A few weeks after her brain surgery, she had a radiation treatment, which was quite an ordeal. First the neurosurgeon, Dr. Hall, screwed a frame onto her head. The frame was a metal halo-like affair that encircled her head about mid-nose. Perpendicular to the halo were four metal "popsicle sticks," two in front and two in back, each of which was secured at the top by a screw through the skin with a torque-wrench-like gadget to find a purchase on the skull itself. Even with numbing medication, it was not a pleasant procedure and, with the frame in place, she looked like something out of a sci-fi movie. But, the frame was necessary in order to hold her head firmly in place for the initial CT scan and the succeeding radiation treatment because the focused radiation had to be very precise. She could not move her head even one millimeter without jeopardizing the effectiveness of the treatment. Using the CT scan pictures, a team of doctors agreed on how best to proceed and the radiation was then quickly completed and the frame removed.

Dani's major complaint during the weeks following surgery was that she had no energy. She was unable to get any prolonged sleep, so she often was up prowling all night long. Yet, she felt as though she were in a drug-induced stupor from her steroid medication and was able to be only minimally involved in family life, although she tried to force herself to get out each day, either to go shopping or walking. She repeatedly asked what day it was, though, forgot conversations, could not concentrate, cried often, and questioned her decision to have the brain surgery and subsequent radiation. She was not the daughter, wife, mother, friend we all knew.

And so it was that I returned to Michigan a few days later with a heavy heart in order to take Dan to an appointment in South Bend with his eye surgeon. At last, there was great news! The retina had reattached and he was healing well. He no longer had to remain facedown and was able to return to work. We packed up and shipped back all of the equipment that had overrun our bedroom since Dan's surgery, with a sense of relief that, at least at home, things were finally getting back to normal.

When I returned to Indy, I was stunned by the change in Danette. While I was in Michigan, she had decided she could no longer endure her stupor and took herself off the Decadron, calling Dr. Yeh to let him know her decision. Now she was back to being the Dani we were all familiar with. It was good to hear her laughing again and interacting with the children, sleeping well at night, and exhibiting more energy than she'd had in months. She does experience some pressure in her head but feels it was a good trade-off for the stupor she had been experiencing.

In the midst of everything she has gone through these past several weeks, Dani has seemed to draw the most pleasure out of redecorating her bedroom and has, at times, seemed almost driven to get it completed. I painted the bedroom for her; and when she was up to shopping, I took her to order a new sofa and select curtains. Her pride and joy, though, was a different sort of framing project from her radiation frame. Dan's mother had saved a number of penciled sketches from her high school art classes in the 1930s. After her death

in 1998, we came across these sketches, which Mom had kept in a folder in a box of other papers, and gave them to Dani. She decided awhile back to get all 12 of them framed to hang on her bedroom wall, along with a quilt her Grandma Head had made, so we picked up the completed pictures earlier this week. They looked great and she was overjoyed with them. They are especially precious to her because when Dani was young, her Grandma Head lived with us for a few years in Marcellus. Then after graduation from high school, Dani lived with Grandma for awhile in Benton Harbor.

In spite of her joy in redoing her bedroom, Danette has also sensed an urgency to plan her funeral, so yesterday we met with the local funeral director. It's all rather paradoxical and is perhaps the best insight into the mindset of many who have been given a terminal prognosis. The bedroom project seems to have given her a focus on the present so that she is walking with one foot firmly planted in this life and the other foot planted in the next. As I used to tell my Hospice families, we hope and pray for the best and plan for the worst.

I returned to Michigan then for a few weeks, catching up with family and friends. In the meantime, my son Glen and his bubbly wife Shelly and their three children, Megan, Kaitlyn, and Bobby, began to make trips to Indianapolis to spend time with Dani. They always stayed in a local hotel with a swimming pool and invited Jack and Daniel to come and swim with them and Alyssa to spend the night. This was a wonderful distraction for Alyssa who was able to drop the heavy mantle of her mother's illness for awhile to play and giggle with her cousins.

Glen is three years younger than Danette, so she was the big sister he had always looked up to. Memories are engraved on my mind of their days together at the children's home in St. Louis, Michigan where Dan and I were houseparents in the early 1970s, of Dani and some of the other children urging "Glennie" to eat a worm, and Glen's response afterwards that "it tastes just like spaghetti." I reflected on the 11 years they spent growing up in an old farmhouse outside Marcellus, Michigan. I could see them riding horses together or laughing at each other as they mucked out the barn and had manure fights. They were always thinking up new games and activities for their friends who visited. As they grew older, they cheered each other on at ball games and kept each other's secrets. Dani's gift to her brother after his graduation from high school was a trip to Texas where the two of them attended a Dallas Cowboys football game, his favorite pro team, afterwards meeting some of the players.

Glen was so shaken by his sister's original cancer diagnosis in March of 2003 that it was several days before he trusted himself to call her. His

quick and fun sense of humor could always make
Dani laugh, so he used that humor now to brighten
her days. When he wasn't around in person, he'd
send emails or write funny notes, and we all were
reduced to side-splitting laughter when he sent his
"You Know You're from Marcellus" parody of the
"you know you're a redneck if..." jokes.

But Glen also has a very tender side, and I
knew that he was hurting for and with his sister and
that his confidence in God's goodness was being
tested as never before. I was grateful for his wonderful and understanding wife Shelly.

Chapter 17

COLORBLIND

Excerpt from MailMax -
October 30, 2004

Today I took my mother out for a short drive to see the fall colors. They don't seem very vibrant this year but, nevertheless, we found some areas that were breathtakingly beautiful. I once read that one evidence of God's love for humankind is that he created colors and then gave us the ability to see those colors.

Recently, I was sitting in a rocking chair watching Danette's husband Kerry as he rummaged around in the refrigerator. "Can I help with something, Kerry?" I asked. He paused a moment, then flashed me an embarrassed smile. "Well, yes, can you tell me if this Jell-O is green?" he asked holding up a single-serving size tub of Jell-O. "Danette wants some green Jell-O." I laughed and replied, "No, that's red Jell-O." Kerry, you see, is colorblind, although he admits to being only a "little bit colorblind." After finding a tub of lime Jell-O, he asked me to find an orange Popsicle.

For the first time ever, I got an absentee ballot this year, not knowing if I would be here in Michigan or at Danette's home on November 2.

As I packed to head back to New Palestine, Dan asked, "When do you expect to be back home?" "I don't know," I confessed. "I'll stay as long as I'm needed." I never realized at the time that it would be three more months before I would see my home in Michigan again.

When I arrived back in Indiana, I noticed that Dani's stamina had decreased significantly. Walking was becoming increasingly difficult for her. Now, even the short distance from her bed to the bathroom adjoining their bedroom was an effort for her, and she confided to me that she had tripped over a root and fallen while walking in the woods with Kerry the previous week. "I didn't have the strength to get up by myself," she said, "and I don't know what I would have done if he hadn't been there to help me." I immediately put my hospice experience to work and spent the entire morning making phone calls to various agencies to line up equipment. Hancock Senior Services in nearby Greenfield loaned a bedside commode, a shower bench, and a wheelchair. I picked up a walker from Attain, Inc., an organization located in the heart of downtown Indianapolis that provides help for the disabled. As I was in the elevator, walker in hand, a gentleman introduced himself to me as Attain's technician. He explained that his job was to customize computers for disabled people. "We even have computers that will talk for people who are unable to talk themselves," he said. I had no idea at the time just how significant that chance encounter would turn out to be.

My next order of business was to secure a handicapped parking permit. After obtaining the necessary physician authorization, I drove to the license bureau, and all the while my disbelieving mind kept asking, "Is this real? Am I really doing this for my own daughter?" The lady at the license bureau took a look at Dani's driver's license and then commented, "She's so young; I'm about the same age. What is her handicap?" I explained briefly Dani's losing battle with terminal breast cancer and the woman's eyes filled with tears. This was not an uncommon occurrence. People seemed so genuinely compassionate and sympathetic when they learned of Dani's plight, and especially when I told them that Dani had three children still at home. I drove away from the license bureau with two blue placards to hang on our cars' rearview mirrors, feeling so grateful that I was able to be there to help make my daughter's life a little easier as her health continued to deteriorate.

Chapter 18

GIVING THANKS

MailMax - November 20, 2004

Greetings from New Palestine, Indiana. I returned to my daughter Dani's home last Monday after she began a rapid decline following a bout with the flu. Before leaving home, I fixed a big pot of chili to take along. When I arrived, I noticed some ripe bananas, so one of my first tasks was to make banana nut bread, something I haven't done in years. Dani was not doing well. She coughed incessantly and could keep nothing down. Her left leg had been so weakened from the effects of her brain surgery and radiation that she was unable to walk without assistance. Her major complaint, though was pain. An MRI on Wednesday revealed no change in the brain, but there remains either significant swelling or cancer. Fortunately, with some medication changes, she is no longer coughing or vomiting, and she is getting around on her own with a walker now. Her pain is gone and she says, "I feel like myself again."

So at this Thanksgiving time...I am very thankful that Dani is once again on the upswing.

The day after I arrived at Dani's, Mary Lou, one of her best friends, came over with a pot of chili and a loaf of banana nut bread. Of course, nothing was said to her about duplicating my efforts because the meal was a blessing and went into the freezer for another time. Mary Lou excitedly told Dani and her husband Kerry about her family's pending move and about her grown children's active lives. Another friend had brought a delicious casserole earlier which provided another wonderful meal. In the mail that day, Dani received a wonderfully encouraging letter from a high school friend who still lives in Marcellus. Other friends have taken Dani's children to various activities or kept them overnight in order to make sure they are able to enjoy some semblance of a normal life during this time of adjustment.

So at this Thanksgiving time...I am thankful for all of the many acts of kindness and words of encouragement from our friends and family.

Tragically, Kerry and Dani received a phone call yesterday telling them that Mary Lou's husband, a

92

respected cardiac surgeon in this area, had been killed in a traffic accident that morning. Ironically, my daughter Cami and Mary Lou's son had been good friends at Wheaton College west of Chicago, so there is a double connection with the family. Now, it is our turn to offer encouragement, and maybe even a casserole or two, to Mary Lou and her family. They are people of deep faith, so I know that they will get through this difficult and painful time, but my heart goes out to them as they face Thanksgiving and the upcoming holiday season .

So at this Thanksgiving time...I am thankful that Dani is still with us, even as I pray for those who are grieving. I am thankful, too, for God's hand of protection as I've burned up the miles driving to and from Indianapolis these past several months. I often marvel that God has prepared me in a unique way through my nursing background and especially through my years of caring for hospice patients and families, so that I am now able to help my daughter and her family.

So at this Thanksgiving time...I am thankful for not only the skill and knowl-edge, but also the grace, to be a support to this precious family.

Last night I took ten-year-old Alyssa shopping to get a new Christmas dress and shoes. She will be singing at a concert on Saturday and wanted to look her best. When we got home, we spent the next couple of hours working on a project for school and studying for a test. The boys are more independent, of course, and are very busy with friends and school activities; but it's fun to see them involved and maturing into young adults.

So at this Thanksgiving time...I am thankful that Dani's illness has drawn me closer to my Indiana family as I am able to share in their day-to-day lives. Truly, my heart is overflowing with thanksgiving for God's goodness to me, showering blessings too numerous to mention.

But at this Thanksgiving time...I once again want to express my thanks to all of you who read my column and for the many wonderful and kind expressions of encouragement you've sent my way.

Happy Thanksgiving!

As I stood in the receiving line at the funeral home for the viewing of Mary Lou's husband who had been killed in an accident days earlier, I couldn't help but wonder how long before I'd be receiving friends at my own daughter's viewing. She had grown so weak and was experiencing such tremendous sciatic pain down her left leg that she was unable to remain for the entire funeral the following day.

Thanksgiving did not turn out to be the happy family event we had planned. By now Danette had been experiencing increasing episodes of uncontrolled coughing, and vomiting, despite being on heavy-duty anti-nausea medication. I would lie in bed at night beside Alyssa, listening to the incessant coughing or vomiting coming from the room next door. Usually Kerry would handle it by himself, but sometimes he'd get me up to administer medication or help with the cleanup. By day I felt like superwoman, amazed at my own stamina and sense of calm; but at night, alone with my thoughts in the sleeping house, my heart would break as I grappled to come to grips with the reality that the final chapter of my daughter's life was being played out. At such times, I'd fling myself into the arms of God, crying out in desperation for my daughter to be restored to health, begging for a miracle, not just for Dani's sake but for Kerry and the children, too. For all of us. But, I ended each prayer with, "Nevertheless, not my will, but yours be done," capitulating to a Divine will and plan far greater than my own.

On the day before Thanksgiving, when we arrived at the hospital for her radiation treatment,

Dani was vomiting blood, so the nurse wheeled her into the emergency department instead of proceeding with radiation. As it happened, the Indianapolis area had been hit by a rare ice and snowstorm; and the emergency room was filled with people who had been in fender benders waiting to be seen by a doctor. I felt despair anticipating the long wait ahead of Dani, but then an angel appeared in the form of the hospital chaplain. Having worked on the same floor as Dani, he quickly discerned how sick she was and pulled a few strings so that she could be put into an examining room immediately. As I wheeled her to an empty cubicle, the scene was like something out of a disaster movie, the hallway lined with people sitting, standing, or lying on gurneys. We waited forever, it seemed, for a nurse or doctor and Dani continued to vomit blood. She turned her sad brown eyes to me and quietly asked, "Mom, I'm going to die now, aren't I?" My heart lurched at her unexpected question, the reality of her condition crashing home again, but I replied, "No, honey, I don't think so. They'll get some IV medication going and you'll begin to feel better."

We waited in the ER cubicle for a long time before the nurse from radiation oncology popped in to see how Dani was doing. When she discovered that Dani had not yet been seen by the ER doctor, she immediately got Dr. Yeh, who came right in to confer with the ER doctor. It didn't take long for him to order tests and have Dani admitted to the hospital. She had been incontinent now for a few weeks, and because this loss of continence was a huge embarrassment to Dani, she requested that she not be put on her own floor where all of her co-workers would be taking care of her. The indignity of it all was just too humiliating. There was a snafu, though, because as soon as it came up on the computer screen that Dani was being admitted, the staff on her floor requested that she be placed with them, not knowing that she had requested otherwise. Instead of embarrassment, though, once she was on her own floor, she felt nothing but understanding and loving care from her co-workers and was glad she had been sent to Unit 6C. I posted a sheet of paper on Dani's door on which I had written "The Queen's Room." And the staff did, indeed, treat her royally.

Dani at 4 months sitting on my lap, 1964

All dressed up for Easter, 1966

Dressing up for Marcellus'
Centennial Celebration, 1979

Cheerleading, 1980

Miss Marcellus, 1982

Dani at the lake, 1983

Dan escorts Dani down the aisle, 1983

Cami, Dani and Glen, Christmas 1983

Kerry and Dani clown around, 1984

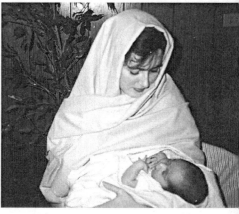

Dani portrays Mary with son Daniel as baby Jesus, 1989

Dani and Kerry with Jack and Daniel vacationing at
Gravel Lake in Lawton, Michigan, 1991

Cami and Dani with
2-year-old Alyssa, 1995

The Shannons, Christmas 1998

Dani as bridesmaid for her
cousin Shantel, 1992

Dani with her family at Christmas, three months
before she was diagnosed with advanced
breast cancer, Christmas 2002

Dani wears a hat after her hair fell out from chemotherapy, Daniel is on the left and Jack is on the right, Easter 2003

*Bald is beautiful –
Dani with her uncle Steve Janssen, 2003*

*Modeling one of the silly hats
I sent her, summer 2003*

Dinner in Marcellus with high school friends – Dani has a "moon face" after resuming steroids subsequent to brain tumor diagnosis. R to L: Cami (drove Dani to Marcellus since Dani was no longer able to drive), Lisa Small Overley, Dani, Kelly McKenzie Reed, Kim Rimes Kline, summer 2004

The Shannon Christmas – Dani is thrilled that her hair is growing back and she feels great, Christmas 2003

Cousins Shantel and Amy work with Aunt Jeri to create a lap quilt for Dani, 2004

Dani on her final Christmas Eve with brother Glen, sister-in-law Shelly, father Dan and son Daniel standing behind her, Christmas Eve 2004

Chapter 19

CONTINUING THE WALK

MailMax - December 4, 2004

Every morning since coming to stay with my daughter Danette and her family, I have taken a brisk walk down her road and into a neighboring subdivision. My usual route takes me about 40 minutes. However, as I return, when I approach the driveway of her home, I have a decision to make. I can turn up her driveway, or I can extend my walk for another ten minutes by continuing to walk to the next stop sign, then making a U-turn to head home. I usually make the effort to continue.

Although I believe that God holds the key to life and death in his hands, I also believe that there are times when he lets us make a choice about whether to continue life's journey. Dani was faced with just such a choice last week. She had been having increased pain and decreased strength in her left leg, prompting radiation oncologist Dr. Pugh to order an MRI of her lower spine. As we sat at the kitchen table after her MRI, the phone rang and it was the radiation oncologist with the news that we dreaded: her cancer had spread to the spine. His recommendation was that she should receive radiation treatments to reduce the pain, improve mobility and to prevent further complications. She tearfully told him, "I'm not sure I can handle any more treatment. I need to think about it over the weekend." And so she carefully considered her choice. It was as if God were saying, "You can head home now, Dani, or you can continue on your walk for a bit longer." By Saturday evening, she had made her decision to take the doctor's advice. Her walk would continue. It was not to be a walk through the park, though. On Monday, we consulted with the doctor about the plan of care and were told that she would have daily treatments on weekdays for the next four weeks. Her first treatment was scheduled for the following day. She awoke on Tuesday with nausea and vomiting, which continued intermittently throughout the day, but nevertheless, I drove her to the hospital and she received her first radiation treatment. She continued to vomit throughout the night and by the time we reached the hospital on Wednesday for her second treatment, she was taken to the emergency room instead. This was the day before Thanksgiving.

Originally, Dani and her family had planned to come to Michigan for Thanksgiving because my brother was coming from Florida for the holiday. We had hoped to have a big family dinner with Mom and my sisters and their families. When it became apparent that Dani would be unable to travel to Michigan, we modified plans and decided that Dan, Glen and his family, and Cami would drive down to New Palestine to have Thanksgiving here with Dani and her family. As it turned out, they left Michigan during the first winter snowfall just about the time Dani was being seen in ER. The weather was so bad that it took them seven hours to get to Indianapolis, a trip that normally takes 3-1/2 hours. Meanwhile, in ER, as soon as Dani received IV fluids and medication, the nausea and vomiting ceased and she was admitted to the floor where she works at Methodist Hospital.

On Thanksgiving Day, the entire family gathered in her room for awhile before heading out for our Thanksgiving dinner at a local steak house. There were no turkey and dressing this year, but no one seemed to mind and we enjoyed our time together. Our good friends from Michigan, Rev. Zawdie and Nancy Abiade and their three girls happened to be in the Indianapolis area, so they stopped by to see Dani and the family on Thanksgiving, lending support and comfort. Today (the day after Thanksgiving) Dani was released from the hospital and she's thankful to be home. She will resume her radiation treatments on Monday and will undergo further testing to determine why she cannot speak above a whisper. She is now forced to walk with a walker and, even so, her gait is slow and unsteady. Nevertheless, the walk of life continues for her, and for those of us who care for her. You might say this has been a walk to remember.

(Because I email my MailMax columns to my son Glen
more than a week in advance of publication,
the following column actually appeared the week before
the previous column in Chapter 19 - Continuing The Walk.
Due to the intervening crisis with Dani's hospitalization,
I have elected to place the article on Dani's
daughter Alyssa here.)

Chapter 20

ALYSSA

One of the most frequently asked questions I get is, "How are Danette's husband and children doing?" Since so many people have expressed an interest, I thought that from time to time I would introduce Dani's family members to you; so I'll start with her daughter, ten-year-old Alyssa. With sparkling blue eyes, a sprinkling of freckles across her nose and a smile that lights up a room, she's a charmer. She's a confirmed cat lover and a fifth grader who is consistently on the honor roll. She often requests that I tell her my family stories, and I am amazed at the mature and insightful questions she asks. Other times her questions make me smile. Last week, for instance, she asked me whether Grandma Huggy (my mother) was born BEFORE or AFTER the Revolutionary War.

What warms me most about Alyssa is her gentle and compassionate nature. More than once she has come home from school distressed that someone in her class had been picked on that day. Her goal is to be a nurse when she grows up, a career which is definitely compatible with her caring temperament.

Since I've been down here in New Palestine, it's been fun to watch the creativeness of Alyssa and her friends. Skylar, one of her best friends, is a neighbor girl whose father was tragically killed in a bizarre accident last year. Skylar is active in local theater and loves to perform. Since Alyssa has a beautiful singing voice, the girls teamed up in September to work up a routine, then put flyers in all of the neighborhood paper boxes, inviting everyone to their concert, to be held on Skylar's driveway. Alyssa asked me if I would attend the performance and, of course, I readily agreed. "When is it?" I asked. "It's Saturday and starts at 5:00 p.m.," she replied. "How long is the concert?" I wondered aloud. "Five minutes," she answered.

And so it was that we made our way across the field that separates the two houses, gathering at the end of Skylar's driveway, along with a handful of other neighbors, to listen to the girls' performance. Even

Danette was able to slowly walk over to the concert, aided by her husband Kerry. I was blessed to see the neighbors turn out for the occasion, and I overheard one gentleman remark to the girls after the performance, "Thanks for inviting us. My wife and I are leaving now to go out to dinner, and it's not every day you're treated to dinner AND a concert."

Alyssa is part of a group called Young Hoosier Singers, under the direction of voice coach Steve Hill. Last Saturday the group presented a concert at the state fairgrounds in Indianapolis, in which each girl sang a solo. Danette had been very sick all week and was not planning to attend, but when Saturday arrived, she was feeling well enough to make the effort to go. Since Alyssa had gone to the concert with another singer, she was unaware that her mother would be in the audience. When we wheeled Dani into the concert, Alyssa spotted her mom and came around to give her mother a big hug, her eyes filled with tears. A short time later, she was on stage singing "Christmas Wish" beauti-fully. When Steve Hill announced the final number, performed by the entire group, he dedicated the song to Danette. There were many tears among the audience members as the ensemble sang the lovely song, "Peace."

Over the past several months since Dani was first diagnosed with cancer, Alyssa has shed many tears. She has always enjoyed a special closeness with her mother. But, in spite of the cloud of sadness that threatens to blot out joy, life goes on for my granddaughter. She is busy with school, voice lessons, ballet, and just keeping up with friends. There remains lots of laughter and fun. Danette's goal has been to see that family life is as normal as possible, and I view my function here as not only caring for Dani's needs, but also helping to assure a normal routine in the home. I cannot erase the pain Alyssa has had to endure nor prevent the pain that is yet to come, but I can be here to love and to comfort this child who is very dear to me.

Dani was experiencing uncontrolled vomiting again. As a hospice nurse, I prided myself on being able to adjust medications to help patients suffering the symptoms of cancer or the side effects of treatment, so I was frustrated now that I was unable to provide relief for my own daughter. When I called Dr. Markham about the uncontrolled vomiting, he said he would meet us in the radiation department of the hospital. He walked into the examining room after reviewing her chart and asked Dani, "What do you want to happen?" Her response was, "I want to be healed, of course. But if that's not possible, I just need for someone to tell me if it's time to quit." Dr. Markham looked at her with such kindness and said, "I'm afraid I'm that person. It appears that the radiation is not doing what we had hoped and it is probably time for hospice." Dani silently nodded her head. This was the moment I had been expecting; but now that it was here, I felt choked by grief and again felt swept with a feeling of the surreal. I struggled to retain my composure as radiation oncologists Dr. Yeh and Dr. Pugh and some of the nurses came into the room to say a final solemn good-bye. They had fought a valiant battle to give my daughter more time, as had Dr. Markham.

Dani was wheeled upstairs to the Ruth Lily Hospice unit just down the hall from Unit 6C where she had served as unit secretary the past few years. Her friend Jeff was on duty in the hospice unit and was responsible for her care that evening. I knew this was a humbling experience for Dani, but she later told me that she was glad he was the one to take care of her because she knew what a good person he was. Judy, a beautiful white-haired lady who could moonlight as Mrs. Claus, was head of the hospice unit. She and Jeff came to talk with me as I sat in the easy chair in Dani's room. Understanding the weight of pain at this monumental moment that was bearing down on me with its heavy, gripping hand of grief, they urged me to allow myself to just be a mother to Dani now instead of a nurse. As a hospice nurse, I had given the same advice in the past to other nurses who were caring for their own dying loved ones. I knew now, though, that for me that would be an impossibility. I would find my comfort and strength in doing those things I felt I did best...mothering and nursing.

The date of Dani's admission to hospice was December 1, 2004. It also happened to be her father's birthday. From the beginning, Dan had been supportive of my many trips down to Indianapolis and of my resolve to remain with Danette when the time came that she needed me nearby; but I hated the fact that he was shouldering his own grief alone up in Michigan. How does a father who adores his daughter give her up into death's grip? From the time she was born, Dani had been an easy child, always delighting her father. She was his basketball protégé and fishing buddy. What memories of her childhood were washing over him as he sat alone at night, waiting for a phone call from me to update him? Thankfully, my sisters who live locally and their husbands, rallied around him, as did Glen and Shelly, the church members, and other more distant family and friends. I put off calling Dan with the news that his little girl had been admitted to hospice because it was his birthday, and I knew that a special evening had been planned for him. My daughter-in-law Shelly and some of the young church women whom I had previously mentored in a study group had planned a surprise birthday dinner for him. When I finally called him, I let him talk first. He spoke in detail of the party and I could tell that his spirits had been lifted by their thoughtfulness. Then I reluctantly delivered my sad birthday message.

Over the past few weeks, Dani had reverted to calling Dan and me "Daddy" and "Mommy," names she hadn't used since grade school. In her confusion about what day it was she frequently asked, "Is my daddy coming today?" She seemed to find real comfort in her father's presence. He was, after all, the fix-it man; surely he could fix this situation too. Dan's trips to New Palestine became more and more frequent as Dani's illness progressed.

Chapter 21

DANIEL

MailMax - December 11, 2004

It is Friday, December 3 as I write this and I am sitting at my daughter Dani's bedside in the hospice unit of Methodist Hospital here in Indianapolis. She was admitted to the hospital again on Wednesday due to uncontrolled nausea and vomiting. However, since being here, the nausea and vomiting has ceased and she is once again feeling well. She'll be released on Monday with hospice care continuing at home. The doctor has indicated that since Dani is so young and healthy apart from the cancer that is widespread throughout her central nervous system, she may live for several weeks more or even months. Her husband Kerry is spending the nights on a cot in her hospital room, while I take the day shift.

The children, of course, have all been here to see her, including Daniel, age 15, who is the middle child. Daniel, named after his PawPaw, is Dani's quiet one and the old adage, "Still waters run deep," certainly is apropos of Daniel's personality and character. A few months after Dani was diagnosed with breast cancer, Daniel asked her, "Do you feel more vulnerable, Mom?" It was such a perceptive question for a young teen. Dani has been spending most hours of the day in bed recently, and it was just two weeks ago that she called Daniel into her room and explained that she probably would not be living much longer. His response was simply to get off the sofa and go to his mother's bedside to give her a long hug and a kiss. When I talked to him later, he quietly said, "I knew it all along." Kerry and Dani have been preparing the children well for this eventuality, so it was not as shocking as the initial news of her breast cancer and then her brain and spinal metastasis.

Daniel is a studious young man and is taking a heavy course load of difficult subjects in his sophomore year of high school. He tends to be very organized and, unlike most teenage boys, his bedroom is always neat and orderly. He's resourceful, too. A year or so ago he wanted a shelf for some of his Nintendo equipment, so he

112

asked his dad for some wood and then spent the day constructing and painting shelves for his bedroom. A few years earlier, with the help of his dad, he had built a push car. It was quite impressive. He also has a great sense of humor and is like a pied piper with a genuine gift for befriending younger children.

Daniel has also been a good friend and confidante to the neighbor boy his age whose father was killed a year ago, as well as to another friend whose father has been abusive. This boy's mother actually called Daniel to come over to their house and console her son after one particularly ugly incident. I am blessed that my grandson has such a kind heart and thoughtful ways.

I was privileged to be present at Daniel's birth at the hospital in Berrien Springs in 1989; and later that year, in a church pageant, Dani played the part of Mary, while holding baby Daniel in her arms. A few years later, when he was nearly three, Daniel had the final lines in a Christmas play. He boldly walked center stage to stand over the manger scene,

picked up the microphone and proclaimed, "I love you, Baby Jesus." Then he threw the mic onto the floor, which made the sound of an exploding bomb, and hurried off stage with a huge smile. He was proud of his moment in the limelight and everyone laughed at the unexpected explosive ending to the play.

Now, like the Daniel of Old Testament fame, our Daniel is facing his own "den of lions," but I know that God is with him, too, through this difficult time. It's not easy, though, for a teenager to face the prospect of the death of a parent. On the way home from the hospital the other night, I commented to Daniel that sometimes this all still seems so unreal and other times the reality of Dani's cancer comes crashing in on me. "That's exactly how I feel," he responded.

For now, our plans center on getting Dani back home, getting established with hospice care, and then working toward creating a festive final Christmas for Dani and the family.

Before Dani was released from the hospice unit of the hospital, Kerry and some of the men from their church group took down the bed in their bedroom and a hospital bed was brought in and set up. The hospice nurse assigned to Dani was an ex-army nurse and seasoned in hospice care. Carolyn came bearing gifts...mountains of Chux pads, Depends, needles, medications, bandages of every size and description. Eventually we had to rearrange the room and buy some plastic stackable bins to accommodate all of the supplies. As soon as I met Carolyn, I knew she was someone we could trust and over the weeks that she oversaw Dani's care, my appreciation of her knowledge and skill only increased.

Although all hospices do not provide for intravenous administration of drugs at home, Ruth Lily Hospice, the hospice to which Dani was admitted, was equipped to do so. A PICC line (Peripherally Inserted Central Catheter) was inserted into a vein in Dani's arm while she was still on the hospice unit at Methodist Hospital. This thin, long, soft plastic tube functions as an IV line, allowing for ease in administering medications. She was now on morphine administered through her PICC line to control the pain in her left leg.

Dani had always been active and she loved to dance. She had only taken one formal dance class and that was after she was married, but dancing had always been a big part of our family gatherings, a tradition passed down by my father. He played the banjo and sometimes a friend would accompany him on a mandolin. We'd roll up the living room carpet and have a great time dancing to some of our traditional American songs like Golden Slippers or Froggie Went A'Courtin'. Regardless of how she had inherited it, dancing was in Dani's blood. She had choreographed and performed in worshipful dances at our church from time to time and, when she moved to New Palestine, she did the same there. Now she was barely able to support her weight on those legs that had danced so many times in delightful abandon from the time she was a child. I came to think of the weeks that followed her admission to hospice care as Dani's last dance.

Chapter 22

SEASON OF GIVING

This is the season of giving and of goodwill and I have never been more aware of that fact as Dani and her family have been on the receiving end of so much love and kindness. On Sunday a group of six friends who went to high school with Dani in Marcellus drove all the way down to Indy to visit her in the hospital. Two of the "girls" had been bridesmaids in her wedding, one was on the girls' championship basketball team with Dani, and all have been good friends for many years. Dani asked me to stay in the room to be her interpreter since she is only able to speak in a whisper now. What a wonderful time it was! There was such warm reminiscing and laughter as stories and pictures were shared. Two hours later, as the friends left, there were final hugs and many tears. Afterwards, I shut the door, put my arms around Dani and, as I held her tight, we cried together. "I've had such a good life with wonderful friends," she said.

Throughout her hospital stay, there was a steady stream of hospital personnel, including doctors, nurses, cleaning people, nursing assistants, social workers, and chaplains, coming by to give Dani a hug, a word of encouragement, offer a prayer, and sometimes bless her with a monetary gift. On Monday, though, as she was discharged home with hospice, it was a particularly emotional day. She requested that someone clean out her locker for the final time on the unit where she had enjoyed her years as a unit secretary. Many staff members came by her room and there were bittersweet tears of goodbye. Many of those staff members handed me their home phone numbers and offered their help. I was touched by their loving concern for my daughter. It was very difficult knowing that she was headed home for her "final mile" on this earth.

Since Dani returned home, her friends have brought over many meals which have helped to lighten our load. Dani's mother-in-law Marilyn Shannon Smart has been staying in the home for the past week, so she has taken on housekeeping chores while I do

Dani's nursing and personal care. I've known Marilyn for 32 years, since Dani and Kerry were in grade school and junior high in Marcellus, so we work well together and it has been good to spend time with my old friend. She has also been a wonderful support to her son Kerry while here.

In the late 1960s while Dan was attending Bible school in Grand Rapids, we became best friends with John Hall, a seminary student, and his wife Marcia. Marcia soon became my babysitter for Danette and Glen while I worked as a secretary in a large law firm. Now John and Marcia live in the Indianapolis area, so they graciously opened their home to me so that I could spend nights there to give Marilyn time alone with Kerry and Dani and the children.

My own sisters and mother have kept in touch with me as I have now been down here for nearly six weeks, offering their help and support. They have sent gifts and casseroles to Dani via Dan, and my sister Carol made Christmas ornaments with Dani's picture on them so that church members and others can hang them on their Christmas trees as a reminder to pray for Dani. My daughter Cami's church fellowship group in Chicago is doing the family Christmas shopping, which was a huge burden lifted from Kerry and Dani. When Dan came from home yesterday for a four-day visit, he brought a bag filled with cards and notes from many of you readers. How blessed I feel! Perhaps in time I will get each one answered, but for now, please know that your words of encouragement were timely and I am thankful for the effort you took to write me.

Tomorrow (it's Dec. 10 as I write this), Dan and I will put up the Christmas tree for the family and decorate the house. In the evening, we'll take Dani out to see the Christmas lights and she is hoping that she feels up to attending Alyssa's singing performance in a local church on Sunday.

May each of you enjoy this wonderful season of love, giving, and goodwill.

119

While I was staying with our friends John and Marcia Hall, I learned that their daughter Marlene's house in the nearby little town of Wanamaker would soon be empty because Marlene was getting married, so I suggested that I rent the house from her, benefiting us both. Marlene readily agreed. After Kerry's mother left to return to Florida, I did not move back into the Shannon home but set up housekeeping in the Wanamaker house. What a blessing that was! I spent the days with Dani and then went "home" to Wanamaker each evening. This gave Dani and her family time for themselves and it gave me the opportunity to recoup and get a good night's sleep. For my entire lifetime, I had been a light sleeper, but amazingly sleep now came easily to me. From time to time as I sensed that Kerry was growing weary, I would spend the night in Dani's room so that he could get some much-needed rest. Occasionally, I would get an S.O.S. call from him, so I'd go rushing over to help with whatever the need might be.

Every morning when I left my temporary home in Wanamaker on my way back to Dani's, I'd stop at a local gas station to get my "fix" of French vanilla coffee and to chat with the handsome young Indian clerk. As we became acquainted, I told him about Danette and he told me with great sadness about his 23-year-old sister who had died the previous year. "I'm still not over it," he said, proudly pulling a picture of his beautiful sister from his wallet. I was reminded forcefully as she smiled back at me from the glossy photo that I was not the only person ever to endure tragedy. It sometimes felt that way, though, when I was in the midst of it.

One of the special blessings of this time was a quilt. All of my Michigan sisters and many of my nieces gathered together in my sister Jeri's home to put together a lap quilt for Dani. It was their final labor of love for their niece and cousin. They had photos from Dani's life transferred onto fabric squares, which they then pieced together. It was a special moment for Dani when they presented her with the quilt after driving to New Palestine, and it covered her bed throughout the remainder of her illness. It turned out to be a wonderful conversation piece. Many of the flood of people who came to visit Dani who might otherwise have found it difficult to know just what to say, found the quilt an immediate focus for conversation as Dani whispered the significance of each picture. Another special blessing during this time was that my sister Carol began to make frequent trips down to Indiana to spend time with me. On one such occasion she gave me a cell phone, an unexpected and thoughtful gift from her husband Ken that allowed me to be in easy contact with my Michigan and Chicago family, as well as with Kerry.

During these weeks after Dani was admitted to hospice, her sons' lives seemed to continue in a normal pattern, but the boys usually popped in after school or work to talk briefly with Dani before taking off to spend time with friends. Alyssa, though, often found it difficult to go to school, so she was allowed to stay home on those days. We reasoned that she was owed the opportunity to spend as much time as possible with her mother while she could. I can still remember her lying in the hospital bed next to her mother during one of the nurse's visits.

Alyssa's beautiful blue eyes took in everything Carolyn did and I think it helped her to know that her mother was in good hands.

When Robin, the hospice social worker, made her initial visit to Dani, I told her about my chance encounter with the man from Attain who provides computers for disabled people. She immediately made arrangements to secure a computer from Attain for Dani's use to help her in communicating now that she was only able to speak in a hoarse whisper. Dani would type her comments into the computer, then press the "talk" button and a computerized voice would speak out whatever she wanted to say. This was a handy device when she felt too weak to talk, but she usually continued to make the effort to speak. Robin visited often with Dani, always concerned about how the family was doing; and Gordon, the chaplain, also made a visit to the home to offer spiritual support and pray with us.

Danette's small church group had been wonderfully supportive with practical help throughout Dani's battle with cancer, but now that she was home for the final days of her life, they stepped up their efforts with visits, cleaning, bringing in meals, running errands, or taking Alyssa into their homes to play with their own children. Dani's best friends Beth, a gentle teddy-bear of a woman, and Julie, who had helped Dani redecorate her home, always went the extra mile and they became very special to me in the process.

As cards and letters, some with photos of smiling families, poured in, Dani savored each one, taping pictures to the side rail of her hospital bed so that she could readily see them. She wanted to answer each letter but, in the end, she simply lacked the strength to do so. She was adamant, though, about seeing one task through. The brother of Cami's roommate Julene was serving in Iraq at the time and Dani wanted to send a package to him. I went shopping to purchase items that his family thought he would enjoy and together Dani and I boxed them. She was so excited about doing this and never knew that the box did not arrive until after her death a month later.

The times I spent with Dani were precious times. It was a time of life review for her, a time of assessing her worth. Although she couldn't talk easily or at length, she expressed her fears and grief openly. One time she looked at me tearfully and with anguish said, "I haven't done anything with my life." Then she let out the little whispered snort that was now the closest thing she could approximate to a laugh and sheepishly said, "What if no one shows up at my funeral? What if there are no flowers? I know it's silly to think of it at this point, but I just feel like I did so little with my life."

I held her close for a minute and then said, "Honey, you have three beautiful children who are going to be just fine because you have been such a wonderful mother. The social worker Robin tells me that she can hardly walk down the halls of the hospital without someone snagging her to ask how you are doing. You have had a bigger impact on people's lives than you'll ever know in this life. And, your life continues to impact hundreds, maybe thousands of others as you have allowed me to share your story in my emails and through my MailMax columns."

"But I feel like a failure," she persisted.

"Here I am dying of cancer when my faith tells me that God heals. Did I do something wrong that God is not hearing me? Death is my enemy and I am losing the battle."

"That would be true," I responded, "if this life on earth is all there is. But you will continue your life even after death and that's where your victory lies. You have looked death square in the face and still you have clung to your faith and continue to proclaim that God is good. Your physical body may be losing the battle, but your spirit is winning by a wide margin...And, NO, you are not dying because you've done something wrong!"

One evening in early December I was sitting in the living room adjacent to Dani's bedroom alone with my thoughts, believing Dani to be asleep. Kerry had gone somewhere with the children and the house was dark and quiet. Then I heard her call me in her raspy voice. "Come and sing with me," she said. And so I sat on the new sofa in her room and, with throat tight with emotion, sang many of the old hymns, as she joined in with fervent whispers. I was surprised that she even remembered the songs since our church usually sings the more contemporary songs. As we sang together there in the dark, mother and daughter serenading the night, a peaceful and beautiful Presence seemed to fill the room and our hearts. Silent night. Holy night.

Chapter 23

JACK!

At age 17, Jack is my oldest grandchild. I recall vividly how Danette let me know that she was pregnant with her first child. At the time, she and her husband Kerry were living in Benton Harbor, Michigan. She had told me a few days earlier that she might be pregnant and had made an appointment with the doctor for a pregnancy test. Everyone was keeping a damper on hopes since there had been several earlier disappointments. On the sunny June day when she was scheduled to see the doctor, I was sitting in my car at the intersection of Napier and M-139, waiting for the light to turn green, when I suddenly spotted Dani's little red Ford Tempo rounding the far corner. She was beaming through her window at me and flashed me a "thumbs up" signal. Jack was born on a cold winter day in February and life has never been quite the same.

Jack! He's an exclamation point in motion...energy plus...and his room reflects his personality because it usually looks like a war zone with clothes, books, and papers haphazardly landing wherever he discards them. His guitar rests on a stand near his closet and a computer sits on a desk in another corner. On the rare occasions when he deigns to clean his room, it's a shock to all of us to see that he actually has a blue carpet beneath the normal accumulation of clutter.

Jack is an honor roll student, but he also has an outrageous sense of humor that occasionally gets him into trouble with his teachers. On the flip side of that, he is also deeply sensitive and caring and often performs community service projects for others. He holds down a job at a local supermarket and recently received a letter of commendation from the head of the supermarket chain because of the good reports received from customers. He drives to and from work and school in his trusty but rusty '88 heavy-half ton four-wheel-drive pick-up truck, which is his baby, and also likes to take it out in the fields to go "mud boggin'." Jack is also "lead screamer" (his words, not mine) in a locally popular garage band called Skies of Unrest. When the band performs, I can understand none of Jack's words, but the fans seem to know them well. I guess it's a generation gap thing. However, I was honored when Jack invited me, his old granny, to attend a practice session last spring; and some of the lyrics Jack has written have actually impressed me with their depth, especially the lyrics to his song entitled, "The Will to Endure."

This is a difficult year of change for Jack. Not only is he facing the coming loss of his mother, but he will graduate from high school in May and has been experiencing the typical angst of every graduating senior as he wonders what the future holds. He has been accepted by two colleges so far and may apply to more but isn't really sure what profession to pursue. When Jack was in first grade, he came home from school one day and told his mother, "My teacher said I might be President someday."

"Well, you just tell your teacher he's prophetic," Dani responded.

A few days later, Dani and Jack were laughing about something when he said, "Oh, Mom, you're pathetic!"

Surprised at the vocabulary of her first-grader, Dani exclaimed, "Jack! Where did you learn that word?"

"From you," he answered. "You told me to tell my teacher he's pathetic."

"And did you?" she questioned with a growing sense of uneasiness.

"Uh huh," he replied.

As it turns out, the teacher may have been prophetic after all, for Jack has a keen interest in politics that is rare for a young man his age. I've been impressed as I've listened in when he asks his father astute questions regarding politics and offers his own political opinions.

Though this is a difficult and painful time for Jack, he has retained his sense of humor and can make his mother (and all of us) laugh with his goofy good-natured humor. He also has a strong faith and I think he'll be okay for, as his own lyrics proclaim, he has the "will to endure."

127

The mood of the Christmas season, at least for the adults, was a somber can-we-just-get-this-over-with feeling. Of course, we all put forth the effort to try to assure that the children had the best Christmas possible. One evening, a week or so before Christmas, Harrison and Martha, friends of Kerry and Danette from Africa, prepared and brought a typical Kenyan meal. It was a feast, really; and as the two families sat together around the Shannon dinner table, there was so much conversation and laughter that an outsider coming in would have thought it was a normal scene. Dani was listening from her bed in her bedroom, too weak to come to the table. Kerry, though, had thoughtfully seen to it that someone was always sitting with Dani in her room during meal-times so that she would not feel quite so alone.

After the meal that evening, Harrison and Martha went to Danette's bedside and there Harrison stretched his hands above the bed and began to sing over Dani in his native tongue. The song went on for perhaps 20 minutes or more, but it was hauntingly beautiful and seemed somehow hallowed.

On the Sunday morning before Christmas, Dani's entire church group arrived with goodies and held their worship service and a time of fellowship in the Shannon living room. Dani remained in bed, and Cami and I sat on the sofa in her room to keep her company. It was a bittersweet time as we all sang the familiar Christmas carols and once again listened to the Christmas story. Uppermost in everyone's minds was the knowledge that this was the last Christmas worship service we would ever have with Dani...in this life anyway.

Chapter 24

KERRY

Kerry Jack Shannon and Danette Michelle Head were married on a hot, humid July day in 1983 in a beautiful outdoor ceremony at a golf course in St. Joseph, Michigan. As they said their vows, "'Til death do us part," neither of them could have envisioned that Dani's life would be cut short by cancer. Dani and Kerry had known each other for many years because, when Dan and I first moved to Marcellus the day after Christmas 1972, we were members of a small fledgling church that Kerry's family was instrumental in birthing. Dani was in fourth grade; Kerry was a tenth-grader.

After their marriage, the couple lived in Benton Harbor and Kerry worked at Mittler, Dani at All-Phase Electric. In the early 90s, Kerry served as a Benton Harbor city commissioner, part of the so-called Wolf Pack. He took his public charge seriously and spent countless hours studying the issues and listening to the citizens of Benton Harbor. It seemed at the time like progress in the city was being made, so it was a real disappointment when he was defeated in the next election.

A short time later, Johnny Hall, a friend who was in the saddle-making business in New Palestine, Indiana, encouraged Kerry to come and learn the trade. And so it was that in the summer of 1994, Kerry and Dani relocated to New Palestine with their three children to start out on a new venture. Two years later, Kerry Jack Custom Saddles was born. Kerry works out of a garage workshop attached to their home and his saddles have been ordered by aficionados throughout the world who appreciate his quality workmanship.

Working right here in the home has been both a blessing and a curse during Dani's illness. On the plus side, Dani is able to communicate with him through a monitor and he is at hand to help her whenever she needs him. On the down side, Kerry has had to field a mountain of phone calls from friends and relatives wanting to know how Dani and the family are doing. Additionally, the house has been like Grand Central Station with visits from those who love Dani and want to spend some time with her. Kerry welcomes all of the calls and visits which have been a great blessing and encouragement but, at the same time, it takes him from his work. And then there is the added factor that most men facing the loss of a spouse are able to get away and go to work each day where, for a few hours, they have a respite of sorts from the intensity of caregiving.

Dani has often described Kerry as a strong person...and he is. I have watched in admiration as he has taken on the role of caregiver. He seems to have limitless patience, even when he has been up half the night caring for her needs and his world seems out of control. He has learned to give her IV infusions and, when I'm not around, he becomes chief cook and bottle washer, chauffeur, and laundry person.

He is a truly dedicated and involved father who has done a wonderful job, along with Dani, of preparing the children for what lies ahead and of making sure that they have as normal and joy-filled a life as is possible right now. Yesterday was a prime example. Indianapolis had an unprecedented blizzard, and as I was caring for Dani in the after-

noon, I looked out the window and saw that Kerry was giving his children, Glen's children, and the cousins from Florida the time of their lives as he pulled them through the snow on upturned trash can lids. His sons Jack and Daniel would periodically surprise the younger children by jumping out from behind snow mounds and mock wrestling, eliciting squeals of delight from their rosy-cheeked audience.

In the evening, we celebrated an early Christmas. Dani came to the table for our usual feast and then Kerry assisted her onto the couch where she lay and observed the festivities. She was touched at Kerry's gift of a necklace, bracelet, and beautiful teardrop earrings, purchased by him not only because sapphires are her birthstone but also because the teardrop represents the sadness of this present time.

I have seen Kerry go through all the seasons of his life and yet his faith in God remains firm, his love for Dani has grown through the years and tears, and I count my daughter blessed to have this man at her side for this final season of their lives.

Throughout Danette's battle with cancer I had been keeping friends and family apprised of the ups and downs of her illness, and I received emails or notes from people I didn't even know because my email updates had been forwarded by others. Every day I eagerly checked my email for responses. They were a great encouragement to me and again it was a comfort to know that people around the globe were praying for my daughter and the family.

During the holidays, Kerry's sister Sherry arrived from Florida. Sherry is a registered nurse who works in a clinic specializing in alternative therapy, specifically chelating and intravenous vitamin treatments; so under her guidance, we began a daily infusion of vitamins. The treatment did, indeed, seem to temporarily give Dani more energy and after a few weeks on this treatment, she felt well enough that she wanted to go to the mall and get her nails done and buy some soft new flannel sheets for her hospital bed. It was a major undertaking by Kerry and me, but we managed to load her into the family van and take her to the mall, wheeling her around in a wheelchair. She was exhausted by the excursion but her spirits were lifted just in being able to get out of the house.

There was a flood of visitors to Dani's bedside during the month of December and on into early January, some came just to sit with her in companionable silence. Some to assure themselves that a past misunderstanding was resolved; some opening the door to the past with reminiscences about funny, happy, or sad events in their lives; some leaving her bedside without ever finding the courage to speak what was on their hearts and minds; some to update

Dani on co-workers and their own lives; some came needing the jolt of seeing for themselves in order to make the gigantic leap from "it can't possibly be" to the reality that Dani was, indeed, dying; some bearing tangible gifts in their hands; others simply giving the gift of their loving presence; all seeking a balm for their own hurting hearts. And so they came, from all around the Indianapolis area, friends, neighbors, co-workers, family. They came from Florida and Texas, from California and Minnesota, from Nebraska and Illinois; and so many came from Michigan that on some days I thought they must have emptied out the entire state, causing a huge population shift from the mitten state to Indiana. And all the while, Dani sat in her hospital bed like a regal queen receiving her loyal subjects and enjoying every visit.

Chapter 25

THE FLOOD

The holidays are now over and the flood of visitors to the Shannon household here in New Palestine, Indiana has abated. I thought we'd be returning to a more normal schedule with my three grandchildren back in school, but we have experienced unusual weather that has caused flooding throughout the area, resulting in many school delays and closings.

It all began with the blizzard that blanketed the area two days before Christmas. When I awoke to the sight of drifted, unplowed snow, I was afraid that I might not be able to even get out of my driveway let alone negotiate the street that had not yet been plowed. Eventually, my grandson Jack came in his truck to rescue me and drive me the ten miles to the Shannon house. Though driving was hazardous, the landscape had been transformed into a winter wonderland that sent flakes of joy drifting into my heart. I was amazed when, two days later, Dan's niece Marya and her family followed through with plans to pull their camper from Texas despite the weather. They camped at a local campground and had an enjoyable time despite the sometimes single-digit temperatures. Marya's children had never before seen such an accumulation of snow and were delighted with our winter wonderland, enjoying sledding in the white fluff while Marya visited with Dani.

As the weather warmed and the snow began to thaw, local authorities expressed concern about the possibility of flooding. The soil in this area does not drain as readily as our more sandy soil in Southwest Michigan and, consequently, most homes are built without basements. On the heels of the thawing snow, it began to rain and has rained intermittently nearly every day for a week and a half.

On Wednesday as Cami and I drove to the Shannon house, we were amazed at the sight of muddy lakes that had appeared overnight in fields, frequently spilling over onto the roadways. Lawns that had been dry and green the day before had now become muddy ponds. On one lawn a "For Sale" sign bobbed like a child's sailboat, half hidden by the murky waters. As we approached the Shannon's road, a newly-placed orange and black sign greeted us, advising, "High Water over Road." Driving carefully through the flooded areas, we reached the Shannon home without incident. A rapid stream raced through a dip in their lawn where none had existed just hours earlier, and the edge of the pavement in front of their house had begun to erode from the onslaught of water.

Later that day, I drove to the local Meijer store a few miles distant and was surprised to find that several roads had been closed due to water over the roadways. Everywhere I went the talk was of flooding and there were many reports of drivers who had foolishly failed to heed the warnings of closed roads, only to find themselves strand-ed and in need of rescue. The news reported that 80% of the Indianapolis area was without power, and residents were advised to boil their water for three minutes before drinking it. We were among the fortunate 20% who did not lose power.

That evening, Cami and I returned to our split-level home in Wanamaker, again taking care as we traveled the rain-soaked highways. The house in Wanamaker is located at the end of a cul de sac and has a pleasant wooded backyard with a stream running through it. Across the road is a man-made pond. The pond was rising ever higher and the backyard creek had over-flowed its banks. When Cami went to her bedroom downstairs, she was shocked to find that the entire lower level was flooded. She retrieved her things to join me in the upstairs bedroom and we contacted our friend who owns the house. We couldn't use the shower, do dishes, or flush the toi-let, but at least we had electricity and a warm, dry bed. The rain stopped during the night and by late the following day the water in our rental had receded, leaving us with soggy carpets throughout the lower level.

In the wake of the flooding, great potholes have opened their hungry jaws, eager to snare unsuspecting motorists. Yesterday, the local newscaster reported that this was the worst flooding in over 90 years. Last night we experienced an ice and snowstorm, so once again the landscape has been transformed. In the midst of all of the unusual weather, we are managing just fine. Dani continues her slow decline and is now bed bound, unable to bear her own weight. She remains alert and, though she does not talk much due to her extreme fatigue and loss of normal voice, she continues to receive friends and relatives for brief visits.

Cami spent a good deal of time with Dani during her break from Loyola University. I knew this was both a cherished time and a painful time for Cami. This was the first time she had ever experienced the terminal illness of someone she was so close to. I knew my own pain, but what would it be like to face losing an only sister, someone who had been her cheerleading and basketball coach besides being the best friend and mentor a girl could have? And even though Cami had wonderful support from her friends, church group, and a counselor, I felt concern over her heavy load. Cami is a strong young woman, a person on whom others lean, and I knew that she would come through the other side of this just fine; but my motherly heart ached that she had to endure the sorrow of watching her sister die. I was glad, though, for the time she was able to spend with Dani and enjoyed having her companionship when running errands and when we returned to our Wanamaker nest each night.

On one of my sister Carol's frequent trips to visit Danette, she brought my 82 year old mother along. It was the first time Mom had seen Dani since Christmas of 2003, over a year earlier. She had had her own health issues and felt that a trip to visit Dani would be too difficult both physically and emotionally; so I was surprised and blessed when she decided to come. She stood in the living room for a few moments after she arrived, gathering courage to enter Dani's room. I knew something of what she was experiencing; I had had the same response when my father was dying many years earlier. Yet I couldn't know exactly how she felt. She had buried many loved ones in her lifetime, including two little sisters, three brothers, a son, a grandson and great-grandson, and three husbands. But now she had made the difficult trek to New Palestine to see her oldest granddaughter one final time; and for her, this was an heroic effort. She hurt not only for Dani, I knew, but also because of what I was going through. Finally, I took Mom's hand and drew her to Dani's bedside and Danette was thrilled to see her "Grandma Huggy." Mom remarked several times afterwards that she was glad she'd made the trip. I was too.

A few days later, Dani called me to her bedside and handed me a gold box. It looked familiar, so when I opened it I wasn't surprised to find the sapphire bracelet I had given her for her 40th birthday in September just before her brain surgery. "Would you please keep this, Mom? When Alyssa gets married, I want you to give it to her and ask her to wear it and remember me on her wedding day." I choked back the tears and hugged Dani tight, feeling her own grief in knowing she would not be there as mother of the bride for Alyssa's wedding.

Chapter 26
PLEASURE IN
THE LITTLE THINGS

Many times over recent months I have debated with myself about whether to continue writing articles about my journey with my daughter Dani as she loses her battle with cancer. I don't want my writing to be a pity party for, in truth, I have experienced amazing peace during the journey and even a spirit of light-heartedness on most days. I am keenly aware, too, that many have suffered far greater losses. I think of the parents who lost not one, but two, daughters about Dani's age within months of each other this past year. I think about my friend who not only lost her young daughter to cancer last year, but whose daughter-in-law is now waging war with metastatic cancer. On a global scale, who can fail to be moved by the mind-numbing losses in the recent tsunami? Nevertheless, just as I begin to think I should change course in my writing, I receive an encouraging letter from a reader, and I have come to realize that this journey is not mine alone...not this family's alone...but it has become your journey as well.

The end is near. Or should I say the beginning is near? Dani shows all the signs that her life on earth is nearing its end and her new life is about to begin. A few days ago, she commented, "Mom, I'm finding pleasure now in the little things." "What sorts of things?" I asked. "Banana popsicles...reading together...soft pajamas and socks." These are a few of the "little things" she mentioned.

Dani also found pleasure a few weeks ago in helping Kerry. At that time she was still able to get around, however laboriously, in her wheelchair. On that particular evening, she slowly wheeled herself out to his saddle-making workshop. Surveying the scraps of leather littering the floor, she ordered, "Get me the broom, Kerry. I want to sweep your shop." Handing her a broom, he then moved her wheelchair back and forth so that she could sweep his shop floor. Periodically, he would stoop down with a dustpan as she swept her harvest of leather into the waiting receptacle. Together they swept the floor clean and she beamed at her wonderful sense of accomplishment. A week or so later, she asked Kerry to wheel her throughout their home. Although he tried to keep it light, her tears flowed as she toured each room for the final time. It was a needed tour. A time of letting the memories wash over her. A time of letting go.

Dani has always been a tactile person. She loves the feel of soft things...a little pleasure. These past few months, she has been gifted by family members with a wardrobe of soft pajamas and other outfits and socks. This pleasure in the soft feel of everything surrounding her has brought her great enjoyment. In fact, one night when she was wearing a new red top her Aunt Carol had given her, she woke Kerry two or three times during the night to implore him, "Kerry, come and feel this. It's so soft." He dutifully obeyed and, having shared her joy with him, they were both able to go back to sleep.

Every morning I read the Bible to Dani and then a devotional, followed by prayer. She finds great comfort and peace in this little pleasure, a routine she looks forward to each day. She also has some tapes with the sounds of nature and soft music, overlaid with a soothing voice reading encourag-ing verses from Scripture. I can hear them softly playing now as I write these words to you and I know they are bringing her pleasure and comfort.

Dani has prepared the children well for her death and found great pleasure in presenting each of the children with a memory box filled with mementos of her life. Among the articles in the boxes were new gold watches for the boys and a locket for Alyssa. Inscribed on the back of each was a verse from Ecclesiastes, "He has made everything beautiful in its time." And, she included a tender letter encouraging the children to give God time to heal them of their grief.

Earlier this week, Dani asked, "Mom, am I going home?" "Yes, I think unless God does a miracle, He will be taking you home to be with Him very soon," I replied. Tears filled her eyes as she said, "My purpose on earth has ended." And so, as her body is rapidly failing now, I take my pleasure, too, in the little things...holding her hand...smoothing lotion on her thirsty skin...reading to her...just in being with her until at last she goes home.

143

Kerry and the children were at church one early January Sunday morning when Dani asked me to help her out of bed and into her wheelchair so that she could come into the kitchen to help me fix dinner. I knew that by using good body mechanics I could safely transfer her to the wheelchair because it was lower than her hospital bed; but I would be unable to get her back into bed if the need arose because she had no strength at all to support herself. I explained the problem to her and she agreed to remain in her wheelchair until Kerry got home.

Dani had been in the kitchen only about five minutes when she said she had to use the bedside commode. "I don't think I can make that transfer," I explained, "but we'll give it a try. If I can't do it, I'll have to lay you on the floor." She nodded her agreement, and we made the effort; but she was like a limp rag doll in my arms and I was forced to guide her as gently as possible onto the floor as her legs gave way beneath her. I grabbed a pillow and blanket off her bed, changed her and made her comfortable, and put on some music. There she remained until the family returned home. Kerry and the two boys then helped me carefully roll her onto a blanket and then lift and transfer her back to her bed. That was the last time Dani ever left her bed.

By now Danette's face was so swollen from the effects of Decadron that she seemed to be a caricature of her former self, and her right facial muscles no longer worked. Her beautiful smile was gone, replaced by what appeared to be a smirk. As Dani's condition continued to deteriorate, some days were better than others. She eventually lost her ability to swallow and began to choke on food. Normally when this happens, there is always the danger of aspirating food or fluid into the lungs, so patients are fed pureed food and a thickening agent is added to liquids such as water. We bought a small blender to puree her food, but still she choked. I bought jars and jars of baby food, but she couldn't eat that either without coughing and choking. Completely contrary to usual nursing practice, the thinner I was able to make her food, the better she was able to tolerate it without a choking spasm. Popsicles and Jell-O became the mainstay of her diet. When I consulted with Dr. Markham, he said, "Do whatever works," so we filled needleless syringes with water or other fluids and she squirted them into her mouth.

One wintry night she was hungry for pizza, so Kerry went to the effort of getting pizza at the local pizza parlor, bringing it home, and pureeing it to the consistency of a thin gruel. She said that it tasted good, but after a few bites, she began choking. As Kerry was removing the food to the kitchen, she announced, "I think I'll try a hamburger and fries." Off Kerry went to the local McDonald's. He came home, pureed the French fries and then the hamburger with water, but she couldn't handle that either.

During these final weeks, Dani seemed to be withdrawing from her family. One reason is that she was now sleeping much of the time. She was most alert in the mornings, but by the time the children came in after school to visit with her, she simply didn't seem to be able to muster the strength for much conversation. She told me that her greatest pain was in knowing what her family was going to have to go through. She would occasionally rally, though, and it was during one such time that she asked for her hairdresser to come and cut her hair. This lovely lady, who had been cutting Dani's hair for several years, came to the house and cut and shampooed Dani's hair, giving her a boost of self-esteem.

Understanding that the end was nearing, Cami wanted to come down as many weekends as possible to spend time with Dani, but she was torn as Danette skirted the dance floor of death about whether she should make a planned trip to the west coast for the wedding of a friend. I encouraged her to go, and then held my breath and did a lot of praying that weekend, thinking that perhaps I had counseled Cami wrong. Fortunately, Dani hung on for one more week.

One of my little pleasures during this time was the brief respites I would take each week, driving into the local library to write my MailMax columns on the computers there. Although I do not ordinarily like to shop, quick shopping forays also became a welcomed diversion. There was a small shopping area in Greenfield seven miles one way from Dani's home as well as a shopping area in Cumberland seven miles in the opposite direction. One day during Dani's final two weeks, I made a brief trip into Greenfield to purchase a book at Wal-Mart. When I approached the book section, I noticed a woman with a name badge that read "Jeanne" stocking the shelves. She was an older woman with dark circles under her red-rimmed eyes and I wondered if she was sick. As I began to search for the book, I heard her sniffling and then realized that she was crying. No longer able to concentrate on finding a book, I finally asked, "Is there something I can do to help?"

"Jeanne" then poured out her sad story. Her

husband had Alzheimer's disease, but she had thought he was doing well enough that she could leave him alone while she worked. The previous day, though, the authorities had shown up on her doorstep; someone had reported her. "What am I going to do?" she sobbed. "I don't have the money to put him in a nursing home and I have to work." My heart went out to her in her great distress and I suggested some options she could explore. Before leaving, I promised her that I would be praying for her. Eager to get back to Dani, I left without ever buying my book. Each morning after that, Dani and I prayed for Jeanne's situation.

Several days later I decided to stop by the Meijer store in Cumberland to pick up the book. A lady was also stocking the book section there and when she turned around, I had a moment of shock because it was the same woman I'd met at Wal-Mart in Greenfield, only she looked well-rested and ten years younger. "Jeanne!" I exclaimed, "What are you doing here? I thought you worked at Wal-Mart."

"No," she said, "I work for the book company and I stock shelves in stores throughout this area."

"Well, you look wonderful! My daughter and I have been praying for you every day. Have you found a solution for your husband?"

"Oh yes!" she exclaimed, "My neighbor was feeling bad because she needed to get a job but now she's going to stay with my husband while I'm working. I can afford to pay her, so it not only solves my problem but hers as well."

She gave me a big hug before I left and thanked me for praying. This incident has been branded in my mind because it felt so wonderful at the time to step outside my insulating cocoon of pre-occupation with my own troubles in order to help and comfort someone else, and I gained a fresh awareness that this principle would be key in healing my own grief in the days ahead. As author Barbara Johnson writes in her book, <u>Pack up your Gloomees in a Great Big Box</u>, "...helping others is a tremendous benefit because...when you refresh others, you yourself are refreshed."

Chapter 27

BIRTHDAY

Some time ago, I wrote that my daughter Dani's battle with cancer has been like a roller coaster ride, full of ups and downs. This has never been truer than during the past few days. On Saturday (the day I wrote my last article), I sat with Dani all through the night, listening to her labored breathing, punctuated with long periods of apnea. Based on my experience as a hospice nurse, I thought that she would not live another 48 hours. But Dani has always been full of surprises. On Sunday morning, she awoke alert and her breathing had eased. My daughter, the basketball player who used to make plenty of rebounds on the court, had rebounded once again. She has steadily improved throughout the week and is now able to take small amounts of water and nourishment.

I was glad that the "game" wasn't over…just a time-out, it seems. This meant that Dani was alive to share in Alyssa's eleventh birthday on Thursday. All three of Dani's children celebrate their birthdays in a 36-day time frame from January 20 to February 25.

Repeatedly over the last several weeks, Dani had expressed her concern that the children have special birthday celebrations. I wondered, though, whether there could be a true celebration for Alyssa's birthday under the circumstances, but Dani's dear friends made sure that it was a fun and memorable day for Alyssa.

Kerry let Alyssa play hooky from school on her birthday and, as a surprise, Dani's good friend Beth picked up Alyssa and took her out for a birthday breakfast with her daughters. Alyssa then went to her friends' house to spend the day. She was thrilled with this arrangement since it meant a day of fun and no school. In the meantime, Dani's friend Julie, arrived with her children to decorate Alyssa's bedroom with balloons, banners, and crepe paper. The look of surprised delight on Alyssa's face when she saw her festive room was heartwarming. Julie was thoughtful enough to bring along a digital camera to take pictures of the bedroom so that Dani was able to see the decorations.

Julie and her family stayed for supper…Pizza Hut pizza and a Dairy Queen cake, the birthday dinner of

Alyssa's choice. Before we sat down to eat, we all gathered in Dani's room where we held hands and Kerry prayed a blessing over Alyssa and Dani. Then we all sang Happy Birthday to Alyssa while Dani directed the pitifully off-key "choir" with her banana Popsicle. Thanks to Dani's friends, Julie and Beth, the birthday was a joyous occasion for Alyssa.

I remember well the day Alyssa was born. I was at Berrien General Hospital early in the morning to be present for her birth, experiencing the awe and joy of welcoming a new granddaughter into our family. It was that afternoon I took my 99-year-old friend Hazel to the doctor, where he diagnosed breast cancer, stating that she had perhaps three to six months to live. Since she lived with Dan and me, the following day a Hospice at Home nurse arrived at our home to admit Hazel to hospice care. On their way home from the hospital, Dani and her husband Kerry stopped by our house with their new infant daughter. As Dani placed Alyssa in Hazel's arms, Hazel beamed with joy and wonderment. It was such a touching moment to see my newborn granddaughter, just beginning her

life, in the arms of my dear friend Hazel, whose life was drawing to a close. Hazel died just two weeks later.

Alyssa's birthday was just one event that made this week memorable. Because of Dani's brain tumor, she is unable to control the muscles of her face. She can speak only a whispered word or two at a time, and is often difficult to understand. In addition, the steroid she takes has left her with a "flat affect," so that the girl with the once sparkling personality now seems emotionless. One day this week, however, I was reading to her when she signaled that she'd had enough reading for the day. I asked, "What shall we do now? Do you want me to sing?" She gave me a long, penetrating look before she forced out the whispered words, "Maybe we should rethink reading the book." This delighted me to no end because I knew that her sense of humor was still intact. (My children have always feigned annoyance at my singing, especially my operatic version.)

Our family sense of humor has been a real gift in these difficult times, lightening our hearts and softening the sure knowledge of what is to come.

DANI'S LAST DANCE

Before this column could run, Cami had returned from her trip to Seattle and Dani had danced her last dance. As a hospice nurse, I knew the signs to look for when death is imminent. Often the feet and hands have a dusky bluish, mottled appearance and the skin may feel cool and clammy. Sometimes the patient becomes non-responsive or is difficult to waken. There may be a gurgling sound in the throat, formerly called "the death rattle." Sometimes the patient will seem to be agitated, picking at his covers or even making picking motions in mid-air as though trying to capture elusive butterflies. None of these symptoms was evident when Dani breathed her final breath.

Chapter 28

THROUGH THE DOOR

MailMax - January 29, 2005

Yesterday, Sunday, January 23, at 7:02 a.m., heaven received my precious daughter Danette into her eternal home. The week was filled with sad and poignant moments, but also with celebration and fun. Dani's daughter Alyssa celebrated her 11th birthday on Thursday. It was a wonderful occasion, made special by Dani's friends who were determined that Alyssa would have a great day despite the seriousness of Dani's condition.

Dani had been near death the previous weekend but then rebounded and was doing better the early part of the week. Late Wednesday morning as I sat in her room, I decided to play one of her favorite tapes even though she seemed to be soundly sleeping. As I sat on the couch listening to the music and watching my daughter, she slowly raised her right arm and began to move it in time to the music. Then both arms drifted into the air, moving about in a graceful "dance," while on her face was a beautiful expression of peace and joy. I sat quietly mesmerized, with a lump in my throat. It is a vision that is etched on my mind forever. Later, my daughter Cami said, "Danette once told me that when she gets to heaven, she's going to be on the dance team."

Cami, my husband Dan, son Glen and his family came down for the weekend, and we sat in Danette's room Saturday morning, chatting and reminiscing. Dani had been unable to eat or drink much, but we would fill a syringe with water and give her a few drops at a time to avoid her choking. At one point, she asked for water and Dan filled the syringe and gave it to her as she requested. As he turned to leave, she pointed the syringe at him and squirted him with the water! "Gotcha!" she whispered. She was delighted that she'd been able to get one over on her dad and we all laughed at this unexpected bit of playfulness.

Then in early afternoon, she suddenly sat up, clutched her right side and complained of excruciating pain. She was given additional pain medication, but remained very anxious and couldn't seem to get comfortable except for brief periods of time. Dani's hospital bed was next to sliding glass doors and as we gazed out, the forty-mile an hour winds whipping snow in a frenzied storm seemed to imitate Dani's own restlessness. Late that afternoon, she whispered to me, "I can't find the door." "What door are you talking about?" I asked. "The door to heaven," she replied. We gathered the family around her bed and prayed that she would find the door she was looking for quickly and peacefully.

I spent the night in Dani's room so that her husband Kerry could get a good night's sleep. I knew from her breathing that she was in the final stages of life. I've always been amazed that the dying process is very much like the labor to give birth. The dying person is actually laboring to expel the spirit much as the pregnant woman labors to birth her newborn. Throughout the night I kept my vigil, administering medication when needed, murmuring assurances, holding her hand, giving her water.

About 4:00 in the morning, Dani finally seemed to fall into a deep sleep and at 7:02 a.m. she breathed in one final shallow breath and in that moment slipped through the door of heaven she'd been seeking. Kerry gathered the children and, as they cried and held one another at her bedside, he prayed with them. Then Cami and I performed one final act of love, bathing and dressing Dani in preparation for the funeral home. Dan and Glen and his family arrived shortly and stood at her bedside letting the tears of grief flow. When the hospice nurse on call arrived, we joined hands in a circle around Dani on her deathbed and the nurse prayed a wonderful prayer of peace, after which we sang, "We are Standing on Holy Ground." As I stared out the bedroom window, I was struck by the fact that last night's storm had passed, replaced by a beautiful peaceful landscape. It reflected the beautiful peace on Dani's face. Though our grief is profound, we take comfort in knowing that Dani is at rest and is joyfully, gracefully dancing in heaven.

DANETTE MICHELLE SHANNON

September 6, 1964 – January 23, 2005

We sat in the living room, each lost in thoughts and memories, as we awaited the arrival of the men from the funeral home. When they entered the house, they disappeared into Dani's room and shut the door. Finally, they emerged, Dani's body on the gurney covered with a blue velvet drape. In her room, the hospital bed had been carefully remade and the quilt from my sisters and nieces covered the bed. A single red rose had been laid on Dani's pillow.

Afterwards we all went out to breakfast. It seemed a strangely normal thing to do when everything was so tragically abnormal. The following days before the funeral were filled with phone calls, emails, and preparations for guests coming from out of town, and Cami took Jack and Daniel shopping for new suits.

Chapter 29

FIRST BREATH...LAST BREATH

MailMax - February 5, 2005

Danette Michelle Head Shannon drew her first breath at 6:31 p.m. on Sunday, September 6, 1964 in a small delivery room at Lansing General Hospital in Lansing, Michigan. It's no great surprise that I was there to witness that first breath since I was the mother who had labored throughout the day that Labor Day weekend over forty years ago. What IS unusual is that I was also there when she drew her last breath at 7:02 a.m. on Sunday, January 23, 2005.

Now I am left with nothing more than snapshots of the moments and days between Dani's first breath and her last breath. There are a few cherished photos, some old Super 8 movies, a few video tapes of Dani, but the snapshots I am talking about are the memories ingrained forever on my mind and heart. If you're here today, you no doubt have your own set of snapshot memories of this beautiful, laughing, kind person who graced this earth for 40 years. Let me share just a few of

MY memories.

I remember a particular day when Dani was perhaps 7 or 8 years old. Dan and I were working as house parents at a children's home at the time. She was miffed about something and announced to me that she was running away from home. "Okay," I replied, "I'll miss you, but why don't you go pack and I'll fix you a lunch to take with you." Soon she reappeared with her overnight bag. I watched from the kitchen window as she headed down the long driveway. About halfway, her steps slowed, then stopped altogether. After several moments, she turned around and came back inside. "I've decided not to go," she announced. I hugged her tight and let her know that I was glad she'd changed her mind. Dani never did wander far from home or from the godly values we taught her. When she was about 12, I found a note from her in my typewriter. It read, "Dear Mom, I promise never to be a bratty teenager and talk back to you. I love you. Love, Dani." True to her word,

Dani never went through the typical teenage rebellion, and I've always felt blessed that ours has been a close relationship.

Perhaps my favorite memories of Dani are from the time when we lived on a small farm in Marcellus, Michigan. I can picture her now racing across the field on one of her beloved horses, Lady or Misty. I can see her and Glen playing school or kick the can with Johnny and Stevie Hall or Sean and Matt McNally or the Green kids. One day last fall, she said to me, "Mom, I would give anything if I could just spend one day running in the fields, carefree and happy like on the farm at Marcellus." I like to envision her now running joyfully through the meadows of heaven.

I remember tears of joy running down her face as she and Dan accompanied me in the delivery room for the birth of Camilla Ariel Head. It was just a few weeks later that I found a note on my pillow that read, "Dear Mom, please wake me up if Cami cries in the night.

I'll take care of her so you can get your sleep. I love you. Dani."

I remember heart-stopping basketball games as she helped lead the Marcellus Lady Wildcats to the State semi-finals. I remember the proms, the slumber parties, the cheerleading practices, her job as secretary to Pastor Jim McNally. I remember her first car, a trusty, rusty old blue Toyota. If you lifted the floor mats while riding in the car, you could see the road speeding by beneath. That car eventually literally broke in two one day when Glen and Dani were driving it out in our fields. Oh, but she was proud of her little Toyota. I remember my pride in seeing her crowned senior homecoming queen and my joy when she was crowned Miss Marcellus that spring. I imagine her now as all of her earthly acclaim pales in light of the crown of righteousness which is her reward in heaven.

I remember Dani as the radiant bride of Kerry Jack Shannon in a beautiful outdoor ceremony on

July 2, 1983. She was a loving and faithful wife throughout their 21 years of marriage. I remember when each of her three children was born...Jack, Daniel, Alyssa. Oh how she loved those children!

I remember the devastation of learning that Dani had breast cancer. In the end, the cancer metastasized to her brain and then to her spine; and the legs that had carried her up and down the basketball court could not take even the tiniest steps.

Dani loved to dance and she recently told Cami that when she got to heaven, she was going to be on heaven's dance team. I hope that once she's run through heaven's meadows, she'll be found dancing before the Lord with all her might. Who knows, maybe King David, that famous dancer from Scripture, will join her in a worshipful dance before the throne of God.

From first breath to last breath, Dani was a special gift from God to all of us. And I am so blessed that God chose me to be her mother from first breath...to last breath.

Excerpts from Glenda Head's eulogy delivered at her daughter's funeral on January 26, 2005.

Dani needn't have worried about not having any flowers at her funeral or that no one would show up. I was truly amazed, and incredibly blessed, by all of the friends and family who poured into the funeral home for the visitation and funeral. As we were riding in the limousine to the cemetery, Alyssa asked Kerry, "How will everybody know where to go?" He told her to look out the window as we rounded a corner. There stretched behind us for as far as the eye could see was a procession of cars. "Yes, Dani," I thought, "your life has touched many."

The day of Dani's funeral was chilly and overcast. At the cemetery, the trek to her grave was a muddy mess over ruts freshly dug into the earth by the grave-digging equipment. After the brief graveside ceremony, as the family left the shelter of the awning, Alyssa looked down at the mess then turned her questioning eyes up to her father. Kerry immediately understood that she didn't want to get her shoes dirty and bent down to scoop her up in his arms and carry her back to the funeral limousine. It was such a poignant moment and a reminder to me of how our Heavenly Father stoops down to scoop us up into his arms to carry us over the rough and muddy patches of life. I had no doubt he was carrying us all even in our grief.

Part II

The Long Night of Mourning

Chapter 30

IT IS WELL WITH MY SOUL

Alone. It was Saturday and the silence of solitude did nothing to quiet the clamoring within. The visitation and funeral were over and the relatives had all gone home. Since Dani's death the previous Sunday, I had felt encased in a bubble of peace and grace. But now, as I sat alone in my lovely rented house, my mind and heart were assaulted by a myriad of painful reflections about the events of the preceding few days...like a swarm of mosquitoes buzzing around in my brain, landing on any vulnerable spot they could find, drawing blood. Unfortunately, I didn't have the sense not to scratch where they bit.

Should I have selected a different outfit for Dani to wear as she lay in her casket? I wondered. Buzzzz. The funeral had been long, too long for people who had given of their precious time to attend. Buzzz. Would anything that was said or done be misunderstood? Buzzzz. Then there was Glen's song. Dani had asked that, if he were able to, her brother Glen would sing a closing benediction at the graveside service, "The Lord Bless Thee and Keep Thee." He wasn't sure he could do it, but when the moment arrived, he sang out in a touching final tribute to his sister. At the time, I was immensely blessed and comforted. But alone in my house, my thoughts were bombarded by the revelation that most who had stood outside the tent had been unable to hear the song...didn't even know one was being sung. Buzzz. On and on my mind replayed the events of the previous days, as I chose to "scratch" any number of disturbed thoughts. My prayers for peace seemed to circle right back to the harassing stings of my reflections.

Thinking back, I knew exactly when the bubble of grace had developed a tiny pin prick of pain, slowly oozing out the peace I'd felt. It was Friday night. The night of homecoming. The entire family had turned out to see Danette's son, Jack, named homecoming king.

It was a wonderful moment in counterpoint to the sadness of the past few days. His band had been scheduled to perform at a concert in the high school gymnasium after the game and the family had been invited to attend also. During a break in the band's performance, Kerry, Daniel, and Alyssa were asked to join Jack on stage. There the students presented Kerry with a check for over $800 that they had earned by selling pink breast cancer ribbons embossed with "D. Shannon." What a show of kindness and support from Jack's and Daniel's classmates! It was a special, happy evening and, yet, I also realized that the leak in my grace bubble had occurred the exact moment Jack walked onto the basketball floor for homecoming and was introduced as, "Jack Shannon, son of Kerry Shannon and the LATE Danette Shannon."

Finally, alone with my harassing thoughts, I called John Hall, a long-time friend who lives in Indianapolis. Besides being a good friend, he has a gift for counseling. I poured out to him all of the negative images, the perceived problems, the "places that itched." He quietly listened to my lengthy litany and then said, "Glenda, don't allow these things that don't really matter to keep you from facing the real issue. You need to let yourself grieve...that's the real issue." I heard his words but my mind quickly defended me...Hey, I'm the one who worked as a grief coordinator at Hospice. I'm the one who's the expert in handling grief. I'm doing fine. As soon as I could do so in a gracious manner, I shut the door firmly on that advice by saying good-bye, with the promise of getting together with John and his wife before I head back to Michigan.

Once again I sat alone in the silence. Now, though, as I thought about John's words, I felt the grief begin to bubble up like soul vomit. I stood and walked into the bedroom, thinking I'd pick up a book to read. That's always a good way to turn my thoughts elsewhere. But suddenly, the anguish spewed up and out, a fountain of grief that overwhelmed and threatened to consume me. I slowly slid to the floor and there poured out the soul-wrenching pain of losing my precious daughter. The tears came in floods. I cried out my grief to God until my voice was hoarse. I don't know how long I sat there; but slowly, slowly, I sensed arms of peace and grace reaching out to embrace and comfort me.

Now that the floodgates have been opened, I know there will follow other times of sorrow in the months ahead until the open wound has healed. For now, though, I am once again resting in God's peace and keeping busy with tying up loose ends here, helping Kerry with paperwork, and spending time with my grandchildren. Glen's graveside song has been a continual heart melody and, in the words of the closing song at Dani's funeral, "It is Well with My Soul."

Chapter 31

HOME SWEET HOME

*Excerpt from MailMax -
March 5, 2005*

Home sweet home. I was looking forward with eager anticipation to getting back into my own home, returning to some sense of normalcy, and reconnecting with my family and friends here. I had all sorts of goals established. First, I was going to get back on the treadmill. I was going to spend part of each morning answering letters. I was going to reclaim my house in a room-by-room cleaning frenzy. And, I was going to allow myself plenty of time just to sit in my rocking chair, stare at the walls and let the events of the last few months sink in and become reality.

Life goes on. Cami plans to come home this weekend and together we will sort through the mountains of Dani's clothes Kerry asked me to take. Both Cami and I are looking forward to doing that and I know we'll do lots of reminiscing as we recall occasions when she wore this outfit or that one. I talked with Kerry by phone Tuesday and he said that he is back to work making his saddles, the kids are caught up in school, and they are all in the process of trying to find a new normal for the family...Kerry says that the most difficult time for all of them is at the dinner table each evening when they are acutely aware of the empty chair.

Life goes on. One of the items Dani placed in each of the children's memory boxes was a CD of the song, "I Hope You Dance." When life gives us the option to sit on the sidelines or to dance, the lyrics say, "I hope you dance." This was Dani's desire, not only for her children, but for all of us. And so as life goes on, we choose to dance.

Dani's death ushered in the long dark night of mourning. Although I had grieved when my father died in 1972 and, as Hospice at Home's Bereavement Care Coordinator, had conducted grief support groups and made countless visits to encourage those who were grieving the loss of a loved one, there is no preparation and no written or spoken words that can totally prepare a person for the pain of grief. It is said that time heals grief, and there is an element of truth to that. Still, there is a need to "work through the grief" too. By that I mean that it is necessary to "lean into" grief rather than run from it; and that is what I tried to do after Dani's death. I once heard a sermon in which the speaker said that if you drive by a house in winter and see flowers blooming in the window box, you know they are plastic. This was a winter season in my life and I didn't want to display any fake flowers of joy and happiness, pretending that my daughter's death was painless; still, I also did not want this to be a morbid time of self-pity. Basically, I just wanted to be real.

All of the clichés that I had heard from grieving families took on new meaning for me as I began the grieving process, phrases such as "one day at a time," "some days are better than others," "just going through the motions," "I feel like I have a big hole in my heart." I envisioned myself as operating in three realms, all of them very real. The surface realm was the area of "just going through the motions" as I resumed my normal life and relationships back in Michigan. The realm just below the apparent normalcy was the realm of deep grief, a conscious awareness at all times that Dani was dead and my life would never be the same. This realm operated the strongest during the nighttime hours when grief seemed most overwhelming. In the deepest realm of all was a bedrock confidence in God's goodness and that all would be well…indeed, that all WAS well.

Chapter 32

MOTHER'S DAY AND GRIEF

Since Dani's death in January, people often ask me how I'm doing. I appreciate their concern and my usual reply is that I'm doing okay. I think it's an accurate and honest assessment of my frame of mind and spirit these days. What I have discovered is that, for me, there are many layers of grief. The overriding sensation of grief has been a profound sense of exhaustion, as well as a lack of ambition and focus. It's certainly not that I'm not getting enough sleep, but grief is work. I find that I have to force myself in order to get anything accomplished, and it's difficult to get out and be among people. Once I make the choice to do so, though, I'm always glad I did.

On one level, I continue to struggle with the reality of it all. How can my beautiful, vibrant, loving daughter possibly be gone? Two weeks ago, Dan and I stopped by the cemetery in New Palestine and discovered that Dani's grave marker had been set in place. Once again we were assaulted by a fresh wave of grief as the carved granite stone shouted the reality of her death.

Every day I feel a cloak of grief enfolding my heart. It's a deep, deep sadness in knowing I will never again see my wonderful daughter in this life. My emotions seem always to be close to the surface and tears come easily, often provoked by the smallest of incidents or memories. There are some deep dark holes of grief that I steer clear of. One is the black hole of "Why?" I know that it's a bottomless pit without answers, so I refuse to allow my mind to head in that direction. I am more prone to skate near the edge of the "What if?" abyss. What if the doctor had ordered a biopsy as soon as she felt the lump instead of waiting for 14 months? What if I had encouraged a second opinion? What if…? What if…? This is the pit that sings its siren song to me, so that I continually have to make choices to refocus my mind on what IS rather than on the what ifs.

Another level of grief involves the pain I feel for the loss that my grandchildren and my son-in-law are experiencing and the uncertainty of what lies ahead for each of them. I especially grieve that Jack, Daniel, and Alyssa must face life without their mother's love, laughter, and counsel. As a mother, I feel deep grief that Cami and Glen have had to endure the loss of their precious sister. As a wife, I grieve for Dan's pain in losing his beloved daughter. I grieve for the death of Dani's future. She so much wanted to see Jack graduate in May, to live to see her children's children, to get her counseling degree...plans that were buried with her on that cold winter day last January.

Nevertheless, I continue to be the same me that I was before Dani's illness and death, able to see the beauty and the fun in life. Underneath and overarching all of the layers of grief is HOPE. Hope that I will see her again some day. Hope that my pain will diminish. Hope that this season of grief will enhance my faith and make me a better person. Hope in God's goodness to "make everything beautiful in its time." Hope for a wonderful future for my grandchildren and Kerry and for the rest of our grieving family. Hope that the seeds of love sown by Dani will continue to bear fruit for years to come.

I know that I am healing. A few weeks ago, I dreamed that Dani was standing in a terminal flanked by two other people I did not know. She cocked her head at me and gave me a knowing grin as if to say, "See, Mom, I'm fine." As I slowly emerged from the depths of sleep, I awoke with a huge smile on my face and a won-

derful sense of peace. It was quickly replaced with tears of loss. This incident, though, signaled the first time that I had been able to see Dani as she was before the cancer and the steroids distorted her features so drastically. Since then, I have been able to recall her more often not as she was in her final months...bedridden, unable to speak above a whisper, unable to care for her basic needs...but as the beautiful athletic gracious woman that she was.

My thoughts as we approach Mother's Day this year have centered on Jack, Daniel, and Alyssa, knowing that it will be a sad day for them. As for me, I choose not to let the loss of Dani be my focal point. Instead, I want to be thankful for the wonderful privilege I was given to be her mother for 40 years. (Her final words, "Oh, Mommy!" continue to give me great comfort, just in knowing I was able to be there for her.) On this Mother's Day, I will celebrate the fact that I still have two wonderful children who love me and continue to bring me great pride and joy. And, I still can celebrate the fact that my own mother is alive and able to enjoy life. I have much for which to be thankful. This will be a good Mother's Day after all.

When I returned to Michigan a few weeks after Dani's funeral, I learned that my sister Alice and my son Glen had organized Dani's Dancers, a Relay for life team. During the next few months Dani's family and friends worked diligently to honor her memory by raising over $15,000 for the Relay, and I was asked to speak at the event in June. Kerry and the children and some of their Indiana friends also came up for the Relay and after I spoke, Alyssa touched the hearts of all when she sang "I Hope You Dance," in memory of her mother. For everyone involved who had loved Dani, the event provided an avenue in which to channel their grief and became a source of healing.

One reaction that took me by surprise in those first few months after Dani's death was that I would have an immediate welling up of emotion whenever I was out in public and saw a mother with her infant. Although Dani was 40 years old when she died, I was instantly transported back to those days when she was a baby with her entire life yet ahead of her and my joy and pride in being a new mother full of hopes and dreams for my baby daughter. Now whenever I saw a young mother with her baby, it always stirred in me a profound feeling that every life, at best, is fleeting and is a precious gift.

In my work with hospice, I have sometimes had grieving family members tell me that it was very difficult for them to attend church after the death of their loved one because of the lifetime of accumulated family memories associated with church. For me, the opposite was true. Although it took several Sundays before I could get through a service without crying, Sunday morning worship service was an oasis for me and I felt a measure of healing each Sunday. I became very much aware of God's presence, especially during songs of praise and worship when I would envision Dani joining in song and dancing around the throne of God in heaven. The words of many songs became more meaningful to me and brought much comfort, especially some of the older hymns I had learned as a child.

The continued non-intrusive love and concern of my church family and my natural family, was a great comfort. Many times I just needed to withdraw, like an injured dog, to lick my wounds. I often lost myself in books. I continued my daily reading of the Bible and inspirational books, sometimes finding solace and encouragement; other times, finding it so difficult to concentrate that I could finish an entire passage and not know what I'd just read. One book that I found particularly helpful was Heaven by Randy Alcorn. The first part of the book is not an easy read since it is more scholarly, but the book ultimately led me to a greater understanding of what awaits us after death. I also spent time reading what I call "vacation books," novels that are enjoyable but don't require a lot of brain power. Even as I read, though, in the background of my mind I was continually processing the events of Dani's illness and death.

Very important to me during this time were the hugs and simple words of encouragement of friends and family such as, "We're praying for you." It was interesting that I could sense very keenly when words were genuine and heartfelt as opposed to those times when it seemed that the person speaking simply offered glib religious phrases or empty platitudes.   Sometimes...most times...I wished they'd been silent and simply given me a hug than try to come up with the right words.   In the Biblical story of Job, his friends came to commiserate with him when he was grieving deeply over the loss of his family and possessions.   For seven days and nights those friends sat with Job in comforting silence. They should have left well enough alone, for it was only when they opened their mouths, that their lack of understanding got them into trouble with God. The truth is that we can never fully understand another person's grief.

Chapter 33

GRACE NOTES

DANI'S LAST DANCE

MailMax - January 20, 2007

My daughter Danette Shannon's life was a beautiful melody, and it seems incredibly impossible that two years have gone by since the last triumphal notes of her life faded into eternity. Since that Sunday morning on January 23, 2005, the song of life for the rest of the family has been written in the minor key, but not without its own grace notes to brighten the score.

One such grace note occurred a few months after Dani died. My daughter Cami was returning to her apartment that spring day with a heavy heart. Not only was she mourning the death of her sister, but she also felt overwhelmed with the effort of keeping up with her classes at Loyola University, her job at a facility caring for children with medical and emotional problems, and her commitments to her church group. As she stepped into the foyer of her Chicago apartment building, she noticed that the mailbox she shared with her two roommates was bulging with mail that wouldn't fit completely into the box. For quite some time the girls knew that something must be stuck in the bottom, but this had occurred many times before and was usually junk mail accordioned in the depths of the mailbox, so no one had bothered to retrieve the obstruction. On this particular day, though, Cami removed the mail, then shoved her hand deep into the box to remove the obstacle and was amazed when she fished out a letter from Danette. The letter had been sent the previous September but had been scrunched in the bottom of the mailbox for months. The letter was filled with encouragement that Cami needed just at that particular moment; and a quiet, warm sense of awe embraced her as she realized that perhaps the letter had reached her just when it was supposed to after all.

Another grace note has been all of the cards and letters from Dani that I've rediscovered in the past two years. When Danette and Kerry moved to New Palestine with their three young children in 1994, though I was genuinely excited for them as they set out on their new venture, still there was a sadness in knowing that I would miss Dani terribly. And I would miss out, too, on all of the little day-to-day joys and accomplishments of my growing grandchildren.

Now, though, I can appreciate the grace note. You see, if Dani had not moved, I would not have those letters she sent to us in the years after her move, tangible reminders of the life she lived. In the past, I'd always been one to throw letters (and everything else) away as soon as I was finished with it, but because I was going to college and then beginning a new career as a nurse, many of Dani's letters ended up in a box or a pile on my desk waiting to be rediscovered during these past two years when I was no longer so pressed for time. Rereading each letter, I could hear Dani's words and laughter echoing in my mind. They are now very precious to me; but even so, there are never enough letters, never enough saved emails, never enough videos, never enough old photos to satisfy our longing for more of Dani.

The music plays on and everyone is doing very well, appreciating all of life's little grace notes as they come our way. Dani's husband Kerry has given up his saddle-making business and has concentrated on ministry trips to Brazil, taking son Daniel with him the first time and Alyssa the second time. Jack is doing well in his sophomore year at college and Daniel will graduate from New Palestine High School in May. Alyssa, my freckle-faced granddaughter, who was just 7 months old when the family moved to Indiana, will officially be a teenager on January 20. These delightful grandchildren have all been grace notes, as we watch with joy the unfolding of their own lives and destinies.

Recently I came across a thank-you note Dani had written to me after her brain surgery. The final words are, "I look forward to seeing you again! I love you dearly, Mom. Danette." What a wonderful grace note these words are to me. I look forward to seeing Dani again, too; and one thing is for sure...I am two years closer now to that much-anticipated reunion day with my precious daughter. Now that will be a grace note!

Those people who were not afraid of my grief, who were not afraid to let me talk about Dani, who continued to go to lunch and laugh with me were the ones who brought me the greatest comfort these past two years. I also found comfort in turning my grief outward by helping others, driving older friends and family to doctor's appointments, taking them shopping, and helping with household and gardening tasks. Although I did not return to work at Hospice at Home, I now serve as a volunteer for that organization doing respite care, going into homes to spend a few hours with patients so that family members can have a much-needed break.

The second year of grief was easier than the first because I had gone through all of the "firsts"...first Christmas without her, first birthday since her death, first Mother's Day with no phone call or card from Dani. During the second year, I felt like Punxsutawney Phil, the famous groundhog who pops out of his hole each February 2 on Groundhog Day to check the weather. I sensed that I kept popping my head up through the darkness of grief to see if the sun was shining. I am sensing now that winter is nearing its end and spring, with the beauty of new life, is on its way.

182

Part III
Afterthoughts

Chapter 34

THE HOSPICE OPTION

Long before I had ever heard of hospice, I was impressed with the Old Testament story of the patriarch Jacob's death (Genesis 47:27-50:13). He's old and he knows he's dying, so he calls his sons together and they gather around his bedside where he gives them each a prophetic blessing, lays out his wishes for his burial, then "he gathered up his feet into the bed and died, and was gathered unto his people." I liked the idea of dying at home surrounded by those family members you love, telling them your final thoughts and wishes. It's such a homey scene.

Unfortunately, for several decades our society had gotten away from dying at home and most people died in the hospital. When my stepfather Ken Hogoboom died a few years ago, our large family was congregated around his bed in the intensive care unit during his final minutes. Even at such a tender time, someone made a humorous remark—perfectly natural in our family—and we all laughed. Dad Hogoboom would have loved it; but the nurse hurried in to hush us. Her concern, of course, was for the other patients and their families. Many times I have thought about the difference between that night and the deaths I was privileged to attend in the homes of my hospice patients.

In 2001, 49.2% of deaths occurred in the hospital, 23.7% occurred in nursing homes, and only 23.2% occurred at home, despite the fact that more than 90% of people say they would prefer to die at home. The role of hospice is to help facilitate a comfortable death at home. With hospice, the focus of treatment changes from cure to providing palliative (comfort) care to a terminally ill patient. The patient's doctor must stipulate that, in his judgment, the patient has six months or less to live; and the diagnoses for admission to hospice care are many, such as cancer, congestive heart failure, Alzheimer's disease, ALS (Lou Gehrig's disease), chronic obstructive pulmonary disease (C.O.P.D.)...any medical condition, in fact, in which it is apparent that there is no reasonable hope for cure for the patient.

Each patient and family is served by a team that includes a medical doctor, nurses, aides, social workers, a bereavement care coordinator, a spiritual care coordinator and a host of volunteers. The goal of the nurse and doctor is to provide control of the patient's symptoms, such as pain, constipation, nausea and vomiting, depression, anxiety, or breathing difficulties. One of the huge benefits of hospice for the patient and family is that there is no charge to them for any medications directly related to the terminal diagnosis or for medical equipment. Hospice takes Medicare, Medicaid, and private insurance; and a benevolent fund provides for the care of those who do not have other resources available.

Hospice workers visit patients in their own homes, in nursing homes, or in assisted living facilities. Some hospitals, such as Methodist Hospital in Indianapolis, have their own hospice unit. The nurses and aides give advice and instruction to help family members understand how to care for their loved one, making visits as often as is deemed necessary each week. Being a caregiver is not an easy task, but it is one that invariably brings a great deal of pride and comfort, especially after the patient has died. I was always amazed to see the transformation in a person who began the care of their loved one totally lacking in skills and confidence, only to become highly proficient in their caregiving role. It is, though, a role that can often be exhausting and demanding. One major benefit with hospice care is that someone is on call to answer questions or to make a visit 24 hours a day, every day.

The aides provide hands-on care when needed, social workers help to resolve family or financial issues related to the illness, a chaplain is available, in tandem with the patient's own pastor, priest, or other spiritual leader, to help meet the spiritual needs of the patient and/or family regardless of religious preference, and the bereavement care coordinator helps families through the grief process through phone calls, letters, visits, and various support groups, programs, and memorial services. The hospice volunteers provide a host of services such as running errands, staying with the patient for a few hours to give family members time for themselves, sending out mailings to bereaved family members, or helping with various fund raisers.

Many of my patients and families were intimidated by the use of narcotics to control pain. There were concerns that their loved one would become addicted, a strange concern given the fact that the patient is terminal. Many patients state, "I don't want to feel 'out of it.'" Then there is the misconception that narcotics are "bad" because the consequences of illegal drug use have caused havoc in our society.

In the dying, though, narcotics are a gift. I have entered many homes where the patient looked as though he wouldn't last another 24 hours because of the severe pain. After receiving pain medication, he was often freed to be able to interact with his family and sometimes even resume normal daily activities. Some studies indicate that uncontrolled pain can speed death. It is the responsibility of the hospice nurse, in collaboration with the physician and a pharmacist specially trained in end-of-life medications, to carefully adjust the dosage of the narcotic to make sure that the patient is receiving adequate relief with a minimum amount of sedation.

Hospice isn't for everyone, of course, but it has made a world of difference to countless families to know that they are not alone in caring for their loved one. The peace of mind that comes from knowing that there are experts available to help as their loved one passes through the valley of the shadow of death lends comfort and strength to the families as they face one of life's greatest challenges.

Chapter 35

THE FINAL PARENTHESIS

It's not unusual to fear death. Even for those who profess a strong faith in God and belief in a better life in heaven after death, it can be a time of great anxiety. That's only natural. I think of it as similar to jumping out of an airplane for the first time, relying on your faith that the parachute is going to open. There's also the very real sorrow in leaving behind your familiar life and the people you love, of having to let go. In some cases, even being very old does not seem to diminish that sorrow. I knew one lovely lady who was stunned when she learned that she had a terminal disease, even though she was more than 100 years old! "But, I was doing so well and I have so many things I want to do yet. Why would God take me now?" she lamented.

Many times I've heard people say, "I don't fear death; I just fear dying." It may be that they fear the suffering and pain often associated with a terminal illness. During my years with hospice I can recall only one patient whose symptoms came close to being as difficult to control as Dani's proved to be. Most pain and other symptoms can be well controlled by some of the wonderful medications that we now have. Patients usually die in comfort and are alert until a few days or hours before death occurs. I think, too, that we are usually taught how to live and, to a lesser extent, we are taught about what lies beyond death; but most people haven't a clue about that parenthesis of time from the moment a person is declared terminal until the moment of death.

Usually, people hope that they will have a sudden death, but the reality is that only about 10% of people will experience death in that manner. Of course, we all have a limited number of days, but when we come face to face with the fact that our time is very short, it can be a great blessing in many ways.

• The final parenthesis is a gift of time for reflection. It is usually a brief but intense season of spiritual reflection and a time of assessing one's own life, its meaning and purpose. It's a time in which to draw closer to God, to make things right with him if necessary and to find peace. For me as a Christian, that means not just living a good life, though that certainly has its own rewards and I aspire to live a life committed to doing good. But, more importantly and central to my faith, it means accepting that God's son Jesus has already paid the price for my entrance into eternal life in heaven.

• The final parenthesis allows the opportunity to say good-bye and mend relationships. There were nine months from the time that Dani's condition was declared terminal in April 2004 to the time of her death in January 2005. (Ironically, I had nine months to say hello to her as I carried her in my womb before she made her entrance into this world. The other irony is that she was born on a Sunday and died on a Sunday.) Dani's last dance was a time in which we were able to express our love for each other and to say good-bye. It was such a precious gift to be with her and care for her during those final months; and though I hope never to have to go through anything like this again, still I count myself blessed to have been able to be by her side. Dani was also able to prepare her children and husband and to say her good-byes to them. If used wisely, this time can help greatly to diminish the regrets that are so common after the death of a loved one.

• The final parenthesis gives time to prepare. There are practical matters to be taken care of such as making or updating a will, including a living will to inform the physician and family of your wishes concerning extraordinary measures to keep you alive. Discussing your wishes with your loved ones can give them a measure of peace and reduce the chance for family friction over medical decisions. Dani did all of those things and, it was during her final parenthesis, that she prepared the memory boxes for the children which they will treasure for their lifetimes.

• The final parenthesis gives the family the opportunity to move past denial and to begin the necessary grieving process. This is not to deny hope, though it may switch the focus of our hope from cure to a hope for a peaceable passing from this life into the next for the person we hold dear.

I continued to pray fervently for God to heal Dani to the very end; yet at the same time I was able to recognize and accept that, barring a miracle, this was very likely going to be her home-going. I suppose there are some who would say that if I just had enough faith, Dani would have been healed. But I have a different take on faith. As I see it, there are the "lesser faiths" (if I may call them that)...the faith that I will have good health or that I will be healed, faith that I will have my financial needs met, faith that I will not meet with an accident...and so on. But overarching all of these lesser faiths, which sometimes *seem* to fail us because of our own faulty understanding, is the unwavering faith in the Sovereignty of an Almighty God who is Goodness itself and who is working everything together for my own good...and for Kerry's good, for the children's good, for the good of each of us. And furthermore, January 23, 2005 was the date God had set from eons past for Dani's death. I take great comfort in this verse from Psalm 139:16, "All the days ordained for me were written in your book before one of them came to be." Dani's was a premeditated death, for God himself premeditated it.

My friend Kathy McNally asked me sometime during the final days of Dani's illness if I felt a special closeness with God through those difficult days. "No," I responded truthfully, "though there were a few brief moments of sensing His presence. I have been drinking instead from the spiritual wells I had already dug during my lifetime." That is not to say, however, that God cannot or will not respond to our cries for help regardless of whether we have neglected him in the past, for he is a gracious God. Perhaps a better example of what I am trying to say occurred in the fall of 2006 when seven Amish school girls in Pennsylvania were shot. On one morning TV show, I saw an interview with a Jewish rabbi and a Presbyterian minister. The interviewer seemed amazed that the Amish community was expressing their forgiveness of the shooter. "How can they forgive someone who has murdered their children?" the interviewer asked. The rabbi's wise reply was that the Amish emphasize forgiveness; they exercise a day-to-day practice of forgiving one another in the little things of life so that when a big tragedy came along, they were able to do what seems unimaginable to most of us. The point is that how we live our daily lives has a profound effect on how we cope and are able to handle the painful circumstances of life that come to all of us.

Often during those final weeks, life seemed so intense that I could not pray except to offer up a "HELP!" from the depths of my soul. Day by day, though, I would find the reserves of strength and grace to make it through that day with an amazing peace. I also had a strong sense of being borne aloft on the wings of the prayers of others. That same sense of grace and peace continues to envelope us as we pass through the dark night of mourning and into the joy of a new day.

The Will to Endure
By *Jack Shannon*
Excerpted Lyrics

In a world of helplessness,

It's hard to find the motivation.

It's hard to find the inspiration.

But we are not of weaker blood.

We'll fight for what we hold and love.

Take me to a place

Where I can rest assured,

And tell me that it's worth fighting for.

Instill in my mind the will to endure.

Oh, Sovereign Lord
©*Glen Head, 2005*
based on Isaiah 25; 4, 8-9

verse 1

He is the refuge for the poor.
He is the shelter from the storm,
And the shadow from the heat.
This is our God, our relief.

chorus

Oh, Sovereign Lord!
Death is swallowed up in victory
For those who believe.
Oh, Sovereign Lord!
Surely, He is our God,
Our Sovereign Lord.

verse 2

He'll wipe the teardrops from your face.
He will remove all disgrace,
For those who trust Him, those who wait.
This is our God, we are saved.

bridge

This the Lord hath said.
It's time to lift our heads.
Surely, He is our God,
Our Sovereign Lord.

(This song was written by Glen following Dani's death.)

ISBN 142512682-0